THE PEAK LINE

John M. Stephenson

THE OAKWOOD PRESS
1982

ACKNOWLEDGEMENTS

My grateful thanks are extended to those people who have provided me with very considerable assistance with the completion of this book including H.C. Casserley, Derek Cross, Paul Hatherley, J.H. Hatherley, Peter J. Hughes, A. Derek Bryan, H.A. Farrand Radley MBE, P.B. Bradnam, Maurice Cracknell, David P. Hawksworth, Gerald Marchington, W.J. Pidduck, Robert C. Sinclair, C.H. Terry, Paul R. Tomlinson, Phil Higgins, K.C. Saunders, Dave Larkin, John R. Gilberthorpe, T.J. Edgington (Technical Information Officer of the NRM) and Alex Murray (Public Relations Officer of B.R. (LMR)).

ISBN 0 85361 282 X

CONTENTS

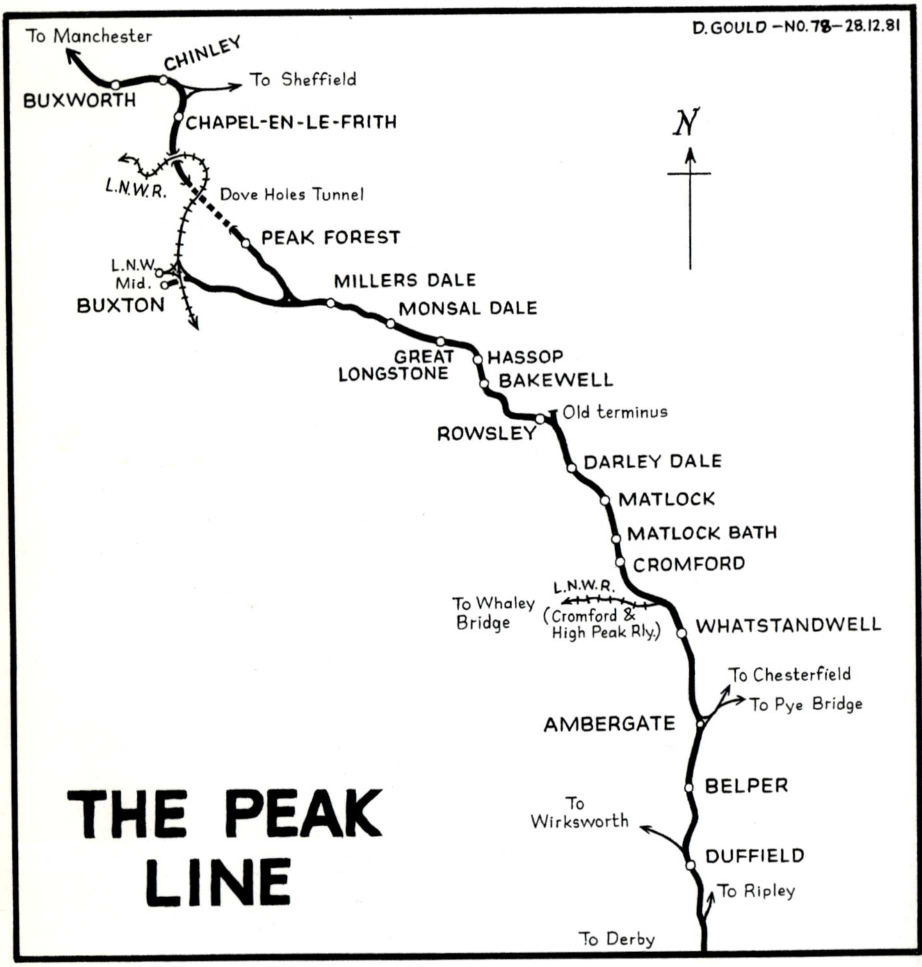
D. GOULD –NO. 78–28.12.81
To Manchester
CHINLEY
To Sheffield
BUXWORTH
CHAPEL-EN-LE-FRITH
N
L.N.W.R.
Dove Holes Tunnel
PEAK FOREST
L.N.W.
Mid.
BUXTON
MILLERS DALE
MONSAL DALE
GREAT
LONGSTONE
HASSOP
BAKEWELL
Old terminus
ROWSLEY
DARLEY DALE
MATLOCK
MATLOCK BATH
CROMFORD
L.N.W.R.
To Whaley
Bridge
(Cromford &
High Peak Rly.)
WHATSTANDWELL
To Chesterfield
To Pye Bridge
AMBERGATE
BELPER
To
Wirksworth
DUFFIELD
To Ripley
To Derby
THE PEAK
LINE

1. Introduction

The Midland Railway route linking Derby and Manchester across the Derbyshire Peak District must certainly rate as one of the most spectacular lines ever to have existed in this country. Indeed it has been described as the most scenic line in Britain in defiance of claims to this title by routes such as the Cambrian Coast line and Scotland's beautiful railway linking Dingwall and Kyle of Lochalsh. Whatever the case, no one could deny that the 'Peak Line' was impressive. The railway was carved through Derbyshire's great limestone hills necessitating the construction of numerous tunnels and other impressive civil engineerng features including the magnificent viaducts at Millers Dale and Monsal Dale, the latter spanning a full three hundred feet across the River Wye on five great arches. Dove Holes Tunnel, the longest on the line, ranks among the longest tunnels on the British railway network. These great structures served to enhance the natural beauty of the landscape through which the railway was forged and contributed significantly towards making the Midland's Derby-Manchester route one of the finest main lines in the country.

The railway was not conceived as a single entity by one company but was, in fact, the result of the ambitions of several completely separate companies who constructed sections of the line at different periods in time and for their own individual reasons. Nevertheless the eventual result of these ventures was a main line providing a direct route between Derby and Manchester through which important traffic, much of it originating from or bound for London, passed for a hundred years. Throughout its long career the Peak Line was used by many fast expresses including the 'Palatine' and the 'Midland Pullman', providing further evidence of the significance of this railway. Impressive locomotives were frequently observed traversing its metals, including Samuel Johnson's superb 4-2-2 express engines, considered by many to be the most aesthetic creations of any locomotive designer, while in later years Jubilees, Patriots and on occasions Royal Scots handled the heaviest passenger traffic over this steeply graded line. Before the eventual demise of the route in the 1960s, Britannias and the stately blue Midland Pullmans gave glory to the twilight years. Freight traffic was also of great importance to the line throughout its history. Following the demise of the Lancashire coalfields during the inter-war period much of the coal to power the industry of the North-West had to be transferred across the Peak District from the East Midlands. The inevitable increase in the volume of freight handled by the route resulted in the drafting to the Derbyshire Dales of large numbers of powerful Stanier 2-8-0s and even the monolithic Beyer-Garratts became a frequent sight as they blasted upgrade through the Peaks with their seemingly endless coal trains.

Clearly the railway was of great importance and with this high level of traffic one might have thought that the line would continue to flourish in much the same way for many years into the future. However, in 1962 the 'Beeching Report' was published and with it the death knell sounded for the Peak route as it did for many lines. Since 1954 traffic had ceased to operate over the Ambergate–Chinley section at night owing to the unsound condition of Dove Holes Tunnel, a structure which had given the operating authorities cause for concern many times during its existence. The years 1963–7 saw the neighbouring and well-known Cromford & High Peak Railway axed and by that time the main line had but a short while left to live. Services were being run down and the Midland Pullman service was re-routed via Crewe over the London and North Western route in April 1966. Freight traffic had been diverted via Chesterfield before the withdrawal of passenger services during 1967–8, the Matlock–Peak Forest Junction section of the main line being closed completely on 1st April 1968. The 'through' expresses were subsequently diverted via Chesterfield and the longer Hope Valley route.

Today passenger services still operate as far north as Matlock Bridge along the truncated spur from Ambergate. Along the remaining northern section of the former main line freight trains still travel as far south as Peak Forest Junction. The Buxton Branch is still open to traffic although the former Midland Station at Buxton has been demolished. The tracks on the Matlock–Peak Forest Junction section have now been lifted but the trackbed itself is still quite sound and many of the important features of the route, including the great viaducts, are fortunately still intact with preservation orders ensuring a long term future for these noble structures.

At this stage one could be forgiven for assuming that this was the end for the former Midland route to Manchester. However, there was always very strong opposition to the closure of the line, particularly from the Peak Park Planning Board. This is not surprising when one considers the fact that the abandonment of the route was considerably detrimental to communications and to the economy of the region. Since closure a number of schemes have been put forward for making use of the derelict trackbed and these include the construction of a public walkway similar to that which now occupies part of the course of the former Cromford & High Peak Line nearby. However, from careful detailed surveys carried out by a number of separate bodies over the past few years it now appears that the most economic and advantageous use that could be made of the abandoned Matlock Bridge–Peak Forest Junction section would be to reconstruct it as a working standard gauge railway providing a full range of services including commuter and freight traffic to serve the local communities and steam operated tourist services at weekends and Bank Holiday periods.

For this purpose two bodies, the Peak Railway Society Ltd, and Peak Rail Operations Ltd were formed during the 1970s and progress towards the reinstatement of the railway has already been made. The Peak Park Planning

Board has given its approval to the project and has even decided to purchase sections of the trackbed. A fully successful outcome to the project to rebuild the Peak Line would see the most spectacular privately operated railway in the country. Time will tell whether this dream becomes reality and costs will be on a correspondingly impressive scale. However, it is important to remember that it would also cost a substantial sum to demolish the railway altogether and that option would provide little or no benefit to anyone. A reconstructed Peak Line, on the other hand, would bring many advantages to both local inhabitants and visitors to the Peak District with the restoration of rail services. In addition the reopening of the railway would encourage visitors to park their cars outside the Peak District National Park and travel through the area by train, thereby helping to relieve congestion on the local roads and improving the environment of the region. This in itself is a very important point and is one with which the Peak Park Planning Board finds favour. The reinstatement of rail services would be a great advantage to local residents during the winter months when many of the roads in the area become dangerous and often impassable. It is a common occurrence for centres as large as Buxton to be cut off for quite lengthy periods during the worst winter weather and the many smaller and more isolated settlements suffer to a much greater degree. It is likely that these communities would gain the most from the restoration of the railway which might often serve as the only safe means of transport and communications at such times. In parts of the country where similar severe conditions are experienced, both the recently reopened and privately operated West Somerset Railway, which crosses Exmoor, and North Yorkshire Moors Railway, have already proved to be the sole life lines to beleaguered isolated communities during the depths of winter. Yet another major advantage to be obtained from rebuilding the line is that direct rail communications between Derby and Manchester would be restored, thus avoiding the present necessity of using the circuitous route via the Hope Valley for this purpose. The preserved Peak Railway would be particularly fortunate in that unlike the majority of privately operated lines it would possess direct connections with British Rail at both its termini.

The advantages to be gained from the reconstruction of the railway are far too numerous to be listed here. Of course, the relaying of twenty miles of track will take many years to complete using volunteer labour as the backbone of the labour force. Tunnels will have to be repaired and stations rebuilt. The huge viaducts, which though basically sound, will require attention although no major problems are foreseen with regard to them. Locomotives and rolling stock will have to be procured at no small cost and yet successes are already being achieved by the promoters of the preservation project. A herculean effort will be required from the ranks of dedicated volunteers who are determined to see the project succeed, but the rewards should prove considerable. The Peak District is visited by many hundreds of thousands of people every year and is surrounded by major connurbations including Greater Manchester and West

Yorkshire which contain a very sizeable proportion of the population of the country. Consequently there would appear to be no danger of a shortage of potential passengers. It is estimated that it would be necessary for the railway to carry about 300,000 passengers per year in order that it should operate profitably, but it is also confidently anticipated that the number of passengers carried will far exceed this figure once the entire route from Matlock to Buxton is reopened. It is also expected that revenue will be derived from the operation of freight services. The limestone traffic of the locality is well known and a return to the scenes of Stanier 2-8-0s struggling up to Peak Forest with heavy trains of limestone hoppers could be more than a possibility. The restoration of the direct connection between Derby and Manchester would appear to offer considerable scope. It is worth noting that only relatively minor modifications would be required to enable steam locomotives to haul modern B.R. Mk II and III coaching stock so the prospect of B.R. excursions and regular services being routed via the Peak Line with the diesel-electric motive power exchanged for steam haulage over the preserved section becomes a further possibility.

The following chapters provide a brief history of the Peak Line from its humble beginnings in the 1840s as the 'little railway with the long name', through its years of pre-eminence as a major artery for north-south traffic to the years of decline and eventual re-birth as the focus of the most ambitious railway preservation project in the country.

2. Early Years: Construction of the Railway

The Peak Line, as mentioned in the Introduction, was not conceived as a single operation but was constructed in stages over a period of about twenty years by several separate railway companies. The first section of the route, between Derby and Ambergate, was opened to traffic on 11th May 1840 as part of the North Midland Railway's line to Rotherham via Chesterfield. The North Midland line was constructed by George Stephenson, the 'Father of Railways', although, in fact, an alternative route had been investigated and surveyed by Charles Vignoles who had built the Midland Counties Railway. The original North Midland terminus at Derby was a fine structure with a large three-span roof which covered the passenger platform, the goods station and the carriage sidings. However, this was demolished many years ago, although some of the attractive station houses on this line are still in existence. The original Derby terminus was approached by an exceptionally sharp reverse curve which caused much consternation to many, including the crew of the Crampton patent locomotive 'Lablanche' which was running trials with an exceptionally lengthy test train. The driver brought the train to a halt because red lights were visible ahead. However, after the fireman had been sent forward to investigate the problem it was discovered that, in fact, they were observing the tail-lights of their own train!

Stephenson's North Midland line involved much heavier construction than other railways generally and was notable for the profusion of bridges and other civil engineering features which had to be built. For example, where the line ran through the centre of Belper it was crossed by no fewer than ten overbridges in the space of a single mile. In fact, in its total length of seventy-two miles, the North Midland Railway possessed two hundred bridges, and it is not really surprising that, as is often the unfortunate case today, the construction costs for the railway were substantially more than had originally been estimated and amounted to the figure of £3,000,000, quite an impressive sum in the 1840s!

North-westwards from Ambergate to Rowsley, the second section of the Derby–Manchester line was constructed by a company with the ambitious and lengthy title of the Manchester, Buxton, Matlock and Midland Junction Railway. This company hoped for much but achieved little, and its plans were unfortunately not to see fruition. The original scheme here was to build a line from Cheadle on the Manchester and Birmingham Railway, to Ambergate on the Midland, a distance of 42½ miles. The M.B.M. & M.J.R. project received considerable financial support from the two companies who should have benefited most from its success, these being the Manchester & Birmingham and the Midland Railways, both of whose systems were intended to be linked by the new line. The Manchester & Birmingham Company was experiencing problems in attempting to obtain access into Manchester from the south at this particular time, so the proposed M.B.M. & M.J.R. line would provide the former with an ideal route to the South. On the Midland side, George Hudson, one of the principal instigators of the booming trade in speculation with railway shares and dubbed 'The Railway King' by Sidney Smith, a distinguished preacher of that period, provided much of the inspiration for the project. Hudson was a remarkable man who had begun his working life as a linen draper in York but was later three times Lord Mayor of that city. It was as manager of the York Banking Company that he began to take a serious interest in railways and took a leading role in promoting the York & North Midland Railway. Soon afterwards he became M.P. for Sunderland and his fame was established. At this period in time Hudson was influential in railway schemes from the West Country to Edinburgh. In the case of the M.B.M. & M.J.R. Project he was joined by Stephenson and the Hon. George Cavendish, both of whom purchased shares in the proposed railway. From the Midland viewpoint the new line was advantageous since it would provide entry into Manchester, or so they hoped. At an early stage there was opposition to the new route, particularly from the Sheffield, Ashton-under-Lyne & Manchester Railway, but in 1846 agreement was reached where the M.B.M. & M.J.R. promised that it would not put forward any opposition to the Whaley Bridge branch and also agreed to assign to the S.A. & M.R. stock amounting to £50,000. In consideration the S.A. & M.R. discontinued its opposition to the M.B.M. & M.J.R. scheme.

But just as the signal was set for 'off', on the day that the M.B.M. & M.J.R. was incorporated, the London & North Western Railway was formed on 15th July 1846 as a result of amalgamation between the Grand Junction and London & Birmingham Railways with the Manchester & Birmingham Railway. The newly created L.N.W.R. was not interested in the M.B.M. & M.J.R. project which would simply provide a source of competition. Thus as one company was born, the ambitions of another were shattered. The M.B.M. & M.J.R., which had intended to run to Manchester across the Derbyshire Peaks, could only raise sufficient capital to construct a railway a mere 11½ miles long between Ambergate and Rowsley and thereby acquiring the appellation of 'the little railway with the long name'.

Nevertheless, both the Manchester & Birmingham and Midland Companies bought shares, the former subscribing £190,000 while the latter purchased a total of 10,000 shares in the M.B.M. & M.J.R., later increased to over 14,000, thereby gaining a fairly substantial measure of control over the line's affairs. For this reason the L.N.W.R. purchased 23,500 shares which would give it an even greater hold on the reins than the Midland possessed. June 4th 1849 was the official opening date of the Ambergate–Rowsley section, while passenger and coal traffic commenced running on August 20th of that year, with other freight services following at the end of December. Three years later in 1852 the railway was leased to the L.N.W.R. and Midland Companies with the condition that they should pay a rent of 2½% on the available capital which at that time amounted to £421,300. In addition, the Midland was given the lease of the Cromford Canal which was owned by the M.B.M. & M.J.R. Finally, in 1871 the railway was absorbed into the M.R. system after the Midland Railway had itself achieved the ambition of the M.B.M. & M.J.R. by constructing a line to Manchester. It was primarily the fear that the L.N.W.R. would get control of the M.B.M. & M.J.R. that had given the impetus to the Midland to obtain a direct route to Manchester and take control of the M.B.M. & M.J.R. itself. Prior to 1871 the Midland had surveyed a number of possible routes to circumnavigate the latter and began construction of a line between Duffield and Rowsley where a line to Manchester had already opened. However, the construction of the link from Duffield was terminated at Wirksworth when it became apparent that there was a serious possibility of gaining control of the M.B.M. & M.J.R. The Midland had also explored the idea of constructing a line through Chatsworth Park, but perhaps, not surprisingly, the Duke of Devonshire was not willing to give his approval to such a venture. The wildest proposal, however, was the suggestion of upgrading the famous Cromford & High Peak Railway to main line status. This would have resulted in the routing of Derby–Manchester expresses over a profusion of gradients and inclined planes sometimes as steep as 1 in 8! This example merely serves to emphasize the desperation of the Midland in attempting to secure a continuous and direct route to Manchester. It was, therefore, extremely fortunate for the Company that in February 1870 agreement was reached to the effect that the Midland would take over the M.B.M. & M.J.R.

Prior to this date, however, the Midland Railway had already constructed a line from Rowsley to Manchester, although this did not follow the same route that had been intended by the M.B.M. & M.J.R. in the 1840s. Owing to a number of difficulties which included opposition by the Duke of Devonshire to the idea of the railway crossing his land, plus hostility from the L.N.W.R. and the fact that by the 1860s the running powers obtained by the M.B.M. & M.J.R. were no longer effective, the Midland had to plan a completely different route up the Wye Valley. The first section of the Rowsley–Manchester line was constructed between Rowsley and Buxton with work commencing on September 4th 1860 after an Act of Parliament authorising construction had been obtained on May 25th of the same year. It is interesting to note that at this time the Midland was also involved with another great venture, namely its London Extension. This was a period of great expansion for the Company with a profusion of new lines being opened in many parts of central England. However, the new railway to Manchester was one of the most noteworthy achievements of the time. The terrain through which it passed was particularly difficult and countless obstacles were encountered during construction, subterranean rivers being a major problem. Non-natural obstructions were also a hindrance. Heading north, after the new Rowsley station the next feature of importance was Haddon Hall, ancestral home of the Duke of Rutland. The Duke was unwilling to allow the railway to cross his estate on the surface, thus forcing the Midland to go underground and construct Haddon Tunnel which, at 1,058 yards, is the second longest on the line after Dove Holes Tunnel sited north of Peak Forest. Apart from the desire of the Duke that the railway should not interfere with his enjoyment of his domain, there was no reason for building Haddon Tunnel. Of the five ventilation shafts which were opened into its roof, the deepest did not exceed twelve feet. In fact, the term 'covered way' would be a more apt description of this structure. Nevertheless, the tunnel provided the engineers with considerable problems and five men were killed in July 1861 when a section of the shallow roof collapsed on them. Perhaps a deep cutting would have sufficed for the purpose of preserving the view from Haddon Hall.

However, one might give credit to the Duke simply on the grounds of his presence in the locality which, no doubt, was the underlying reason for the existence of a far grander station building at Bakewell than one might have expected to find serving a small town in the sparsely populated Peak District. This particular station was actually used by the Duke, and his own personal coat of arms decorated the structure. The Duke of Devonshire, however, used Hassop station which was sited north of Bakewell and two miles from the small settlement from which it acquired its name. The reason was simply that Devonshire required a station of his own in order to avoid the indignity of having to share one with his neighbouring aristocrat. Longstone, the next station to be built and later renamed Great Longstone, served the occupants of Thornbridge Hall. It would certainly be true to say the Peak Line possessed nobility!

Heading further northwards, the railway was taken through the 533-yard Headstone Tunnel driven beneath the hamlet of Little Longstone. No ventilation shafts were provided here, nor at the following Cressbrook and Litton Tunnels. During 1861 construction proceeded on what is almost undoubtedly the finest non-natural feature of the line, the great Monsal Dale viaduct carrying the railway across the River Wye, a structure which is symbolic of the majesty of the Midland route through the Peak. Despite the fact that the local population here was rather sparce, it was decided to build a station at Monsal Dale, to the west of the viaduct, primarily for the benefit of the substantial numbers of tourists who flocked to this beautiful location. The Up platform at this station is notable since the valley sides at this point are so sheer that wooden piles had to be driven into them in order to support it securely. However, the Down platform was a much more solid affair, as was the trackbed which was carved out of the rock. Next came two relatively short tunnels, namely Cressbrook of 471 yards and Litton of 515 yards which remained unlined until the year 1880, having also been carved out of the limestone. Quite a considerable amount of work took place in the vicinity of

Millers Dale including the construction of quite a sizeable station which, apart from the example at Buxton, was the longest on this section. Two huge viaducts were also built here which, like the structure at Monsal Dale, remain standing to this day. When the line was being built, only one viaduct, the southernmost, was deemed necessary at Millers Dale. The partner is a later edition and was opened on August 20th 1905 at a time when the earlier structure was closed for the purpose of having important repair work carried out on it. Millers Dale station developed over a period of time to become quite a significant rail centre and new platforms were added as its importance grew. A bay platform was provided specifically for the Buxton branch traffic. It might appear surprising that the important spa town of Buxton was to be served only by a mere branch line. Unfortunately no other means of providing rail communications were feasible owing to the geographical location of the settlement which, like many established by the Romans, is sited on top of a hill. The nature of the terrain made the building of a line westwards from Buxton an impossibility. However, in partial recompense for this indignity the Midland Railway constructed a fine station to serve the inhabitants of the town. The building possessed a handsome façade which was copied by the L.N.W.R. when that company established its own terminus next door. Regrettably the Midland building was demolished some years ago but we can hope that a new structure will be built to the same design to serve as the northern terminus of the preserved railway.

Returning to the subject of the Midland Railway's endeavours to construct a railway to Manchester, north of Millers Dale innumerable problems were encountered with this next section towards the junction at Peak Forest. Almost immediately to the west of Millers Dale the proposed route for the new line was barred by a limestone spur. The River Wye circumnavigated this obstruction without any problem but did not take care to leave room for the railway builders. However, no problem is insurmountable, or so it is said, and it was decided to drive a 430-yard tunnel, to be named Chee Tor No. 1, into the hillside. This was followed by the construction of Chee Tor No. 2 and Rusher Cutting Tunnels which were of somewhat shorter longitudinal dimensions, Chee Tor No. 2 being a mere 70 yards in length. This tunnel was reached after the railway crossed the River Wye at Chee Dale. Owing to the unfortunate fact that the river occupied all the available space in this part of the valley it was necessary to lay the railway on a shelf hewn out of the valley side for a distance of 400 yards. Such difficulties were more commonly experienced by railway builders in the Andes!

Moving northwards, a triangular configuration of lines merged to form Peak Forest Junction. Here the Buxton branch diverged away from the main line and continued through Wye Dale and the 191-yard Pic Tor Tunnel to Ashwood Dale. Here a further tunnel was bored to the convenient length of exactly one hundred yards. Beyond Ashwood Dale a viaduct was constructed for the purpose of carrying the line into Buxton Midland station. This branch to Buxton was eventually opened on June 1st 1863. Returning to the main line, at Peak Forest Junction no fewer than three signal boxes, namely Buxton Junction, Millers Dale Junction and Peak Forest Junction, were constructed to serve the converging lines. In addition a station named Blackwell Mill was built for the purpose of serving the small settlement of Blackwell, situated about one mile away, together with a group of cottages which had been built by the Midland Railway to house several of their employees. Blackwell Mill station could certainly claim to be one of the smallest in the country and possessed two minute platforms which were barely long enough to accommodate a single carriage. Beyond Millers Dale Junction the main line was taken through yet two further tunnels, their necessity providing additional evidence of the difficult nature of the terrain through which the line was driven. These two structures were named Peak Forest and Great Rocks tunnels, possessing the modest lengths of 121 and 161 yards respectively. The railway was then taken up to its highest point at the summit at Peak Forest where the altitude attained was no less than 980 feet, similar to Shap summit on the West Coast main line. As can be seen from the gradient profile charts, there was an almost continuous gradient rising from the south which actually began at Trent Junction and continued for approximately thirty miles before Peak Forest Summit was finally reached! The relatively gentle ascent through Derby, Ambergate and Matlock gave a somewhat misleading impression of what was to come. From Milepost 149 at Rowsley there followed fifteen miles of almost constant climbing with only a few 'saw-teeth' to provide locomotives and their crews with a brief respite from this gruelling uphill slog. The final three miles of the bank up to the summit were at a gradient of 1 in 90 thus assuring that trains faced a particularly arduous climb which grew steeper as they progressed. Although this presented problems for the operating authorities it did at least bring advantages for the lineside loco spotters since the gradients often necessitated the use of more powerful motive power than would otherwise have been required. The use of giant Beyer-Garratts on heavy coal trains serves as an example here. One of the primary tasks of the locomotive depot at Rowsley was to provide banking engines to assist heavy northbound trains up to the summit.

From the opposite side the ascent from Manchester was equally difficult, if not more so, and included many miles of gradients as steep as 1 in 90 although the ¾-mile stretch of level track from milepost 173 provided some measure of respite for hardworked locomotives and crews. From Disley Tunnel the descent continued at 1 in 132 and subsequently at varying grades between 1 in 100 and 1 in 140 to Cheadle Heath. The final 1¾ miles of route over the long viaduct into Manchester Central Station were upgrade with sections at 1 in 100. However, the possibility of southbound trains making use of this favourable gradient to their advantage was largely nullified by the severe speed restriction which covered the junction at Throstle Nest. The climb to Peak Forest was exceptionally arduous from either direction providing little respite from the upward grades.

Just before the summit, on the southern approach, the Midland constructed a station which they decided in their wisdom to call 'Peak Forest' although, in fact, the village of that name was situated a full three miles away! Having cleared the summit, the line was then plunged into the gloomy depths of Dove Holes Tunnel which, at a length of 1 mile and 1,224 yards, had the distinction of being the longest on the Peak Line. The gradient here was a continuous 1 in 90 and resulted in the southern portal of the tunnel being almost one hundred feet higher than that at the northern end. This structure provided many problems for the railway builders, as indeed it did for the railway operators for many years after. When the tunnel was under construction the contractors had the misfortune to encounter one of Derbyshire's subterranean rivers which inconveniently crossed the path of the bore. The river was subsequently diverted but that was not to be the end of the story since it continued to make persistent unscheduled appearances to the consternation of all concerned. This tunnel had a troubled life and collapsed on two occasions, the first disaster occurring on June 19th 1872, a mere five years after it had been opened to traffic. The second collapse occurred on February 2nd 1940 as a result of severe storms and heavy rain which seriously aggravated the permanently damp and waterlogged condition of the structure. On this second occasion the catastrophe was not discovered until a Derby-bound train ploughed into the blockage! Dove Holes Tunnel earned notoriety from its unwelcome propensity for shedding material on to passing trains, particularly those travelling from Manchester with the locomotives scouring the roof with their exhausts as they slogged up to Peak Forest Summit. The generally poor condition of this tunnel was eventually given as one of the primary reasons for abandoning the Derby–Manchester main line as a trunk route.

The construction of the railway was continued northwards to Chapel-en-le-Frith where a station was built on an impressive viaduct no less than half a mile in length which carried the line across the town. Another viaduct was constructed to cross the old Peak Forest Tramway at Chapel Milton. The route was then continued to Chinley which later became quite an important junction where even London–Manchester expresses sometimes stopped. From Chinley the route was driven westwards to Buxworth which had the fortune to be provided with a station. When the line was originally constructed a tunnel was built here but this was opened out in 1902 when the track was quadrupled along this section. As at Dove Holes, the contractors who built the railway also encountered severe difficulties at Buxworth. In October 1866, immediately before the commencement of passenger services, a huge mass of shale superimposed on sandstone started to slide down towards the railway and took somewhere in the region of sixteen acres of fine pasture land together with a farmhouse and breached the Midland's new Buxworth viaduct. In view of this catastrophe a decision was taken to construct a new line to circumnavigate the obstruction although this resulted in delaying the opening of the route by three months.

From Buxworth, sometimes referred to as 'Bugsworth', the Midland line was carried down a steep gradient of 1 in 98 and through a tunnel, 120 yards long, before entering New Mills. By this stage the Midland was in striking distance of Manchester, the Lancashire border being only a few miles farther west. However, the city of cotton warehouses and belching foundry chimneys remained out of reach for the time being, the company having unfortunately exhausted its available capital for further work on this railway. Yet more problems were considered likely in the form of possible opposition to the Midland scheme from the rival L.N.W.R. and also the Manchester, Sheffield & Lincolnshire Railway (known then as the Sheffield Company and later to become the Great Central). The L.N.W.R. and M.S.L.R. both occupied Manchester's London Road Station and, as well as the Midland, looked upon the territory between there and Buxton as their own by right. The prospects for the Midland project appeared bleak at this stage, but by pure chance matters were to be resolved in the M.R.'s favour. While examining the local terrain, some officers of that company happened to meet several representatives of the M.S.L.R. who were themselves engaged on a similar task. One might reasonably have expected that violent hostilities would immediately break out between the two rival groups. However, shrewd minds were fortunately at work on that occasion and the meeting proved to be far from unmannerly. It was decided that the two companies should join forces against the L.N.W.R. and an agreement was reached whereby the Midland should obtain access to London Road Station (Manchester) together with other parts of Lancashire and Cheshire. As well as gaining this very welcome support from the M.S.L.R. the Midland was fortunate in possessing friends among the influential members of the Manchester City Council and Chamber of Commerce. Thus, instead of being faced by overwhelmingly strong opposition from those who objected to M.R. aspirations in Lancashire, the company found itself with quite a comfortably large number of allies. With help from these various parties the Midland at least realised its very long standing dream of entry into Manchester.

However, this good measure of success in its endeavours did not mean that the Midland no longer possessed problems. To begin with, the continuation of the route into Manchester was not owned by the M.R. A separate company, the Sheffield and Midland Committee, was formed in 1872 to manage the new line. It possessed its own company seal and its directors were drawn from the Sheffield Boards. The Committee took over the route to Manchester, this being only part of its jurisdiction for it was also in control of another line in a different part of the country, namely the Brancliffe Junction–Dinnington Junction route situated to the east of Sheffield on the other side of the Pennines. This particular company was to continue to function for a good many years albeit under different names. In 1904 it became the Great Central and Midland Joint Committee while at the 1923 Grouping its appellation was changed again becoming the L.N.E.R. & L.M.S. Joint Line. The new route to

Midland Railway Station.   Derby.

Derby Midland Station as it appeared in the late 19th. Century (K.C. Saunders Collection)

Midland Johnson Class 2 4-4-0 451 at Ambergate in June 1911 (NRM York)

The unusual triangular station at Ambergate is seen in this view dating from April 1911 (NRM York)

Midland Johnson Class 3 4-4-0   723 is seen at Cromford Station with an up express on 24th. April 1911 (NRM York)

Midland 4-4-0   332 crosses the River Derwent near Ambergate on 15th. June 1911 (NRM York)

A Midland Kirtley 2-4-0 pauses at Cromford Station on 20th. April 1911 (NRM York)

Matlock Bridge Station as it appears today with the northbound track removed (J.G. Hill)

Ex-Midland Class 4 4-4-0. 1062 with a down Manchester express at Matlock Bath (H.C. Casserley Collection)

A timeless scene at Bakewell Station in this view dating from September 1903 (NRM York)

Ex-Midland Class 4 4-4-0 1089 approaches Monsal Dale Station on 24th. June 1933 (H.C. Casserley)

Ex-Midland Johnson 1P 0-4-4T 1421 stands at Millers Dale Station on 24th. June 1933 (H. C. Casserley)

Ex-Midland 2F 0-6-0 58224 at Millers Dale Station on 15th. April 1951 (H.C. Casserley)

Ex-Midland 0-4-4T 58084 stands at Millers Dale Station on 15th. May 1953 (H.C. Casserley)

Ex-Midland Class 2 4-4-0 447 stands at Buxton Midland Station on 3rd. May 1934 (H.C. Casserley)

Sheffield train leaving Chinley with 4-4-0 No. 385, Apr. 1931 (R.D. Pollard)

A scene at Rowsley marshalling yard with several locomotives including a 9F 2-10-0 in evidence (J.H. Hatherley)

Ex-LMS Rebuilt Patriot 4-6-0 45540 'Sir Robert Turnbull' heads a down express through Rowsley (J.H. Hatherley)

Ex-LMS Crab 2-6-0   42874 hauls a down goods near Bakewell on 2nd. May 1953
(Peter J. Hughes)

Stanier 8F 2-8-0 48751 blasts up-grade near Bakewell with a heavy train of limestone hoppers (H.C. Casserley)

Fowler 4F 0-6-0 44101 provides banking assistance for a heavy freight at Bakewell in May 1953 (H.C. Casserley)

Ancient and modern at Rowsley as a Type 4 'Peak' diesel hurries an express past an ex-LNWR 0-8-0 in the marshalling yards (J.H. Hatherley)

An unidentified 2-6-4T from Rowsley shed banks a heavy freight up grade towards Milllers Dale (John Robinson)

Ex-Midland 4F 0-6-0 43914 passes Hassop Station with a down goods on 2nd. May 1953 (Peter J. Hughes)

Grimy 4F 0-6-0 44480 hauls an up goods near Hassop on 2nd. May 1953 (Peter J. Hughes)

Ex-W.D. 2-8-0. 90666 is seen here with an up freight in the vicinity of Hassop on 21st. May 1953 (Peter J. Hughes)

Ex-LMS Stanier 5MT 2-6-0 42956 storms up grade between Hassop and Great Longstone (John Robinson)

B.R. 9F 2-10-0 92012 makes an imposing sight as she climbs towards Millers Dale with a train of limestone hoppers (John Robinson)

An ex-LMS Crab darkens the sky as she storms up the gradient with a heavy coal train (John Robinson)

Following the exertions of a banking turn, 4F 0-6-0 44101 returns light engine to Rowsley through the tranquil beauty of Monsal Dale (H.C. Casserley)

Ex-Midland 4F 0-6-0 No.44024 leaving Monsal Dale with a Down freight in April 1949 (Peter J. Hughes)

A Stanier 2-8-0 trundles a long rake of coal wagons through a seemingly deserted Millers Dale Station (John Robinson)

Manchester was taken via Marple and was, in fact, known as the Marple, New Mills and Hayfield Junction Railway. Work on this line commenced in 1860 and by July 1st 1865 the section between Marple and New Mills (Central) was opened to traffic. Beyond Marple running powers into Manchester were obtained from the M.S.L.R.

The fact that it was not under full Midland ownership and control eventually led to the decision by that organisation to construct a new purely Midland route into Manchester. Thus, the building of the new line commenced at the indelicately named location of Gowhole and construction continued to Disley, the line being taken over varying grades and even a ¾-mile stretch of level track! However, the opening of the 2 mile and 346 yard long Disley Tunnel was necessary before Manchester could be reached by this particular route. The tunnel had the distinction of being the second longest on the whole of the Midland system. Clearly the attainment of a Midland main line to Manchester had been a singularly difficult accomplishment. From Disley Tunnel the railway was taken down a gradient of 1 in 100 to Hazel Grove and thence along the south-west boundary of Stockport. A station was constructed at Cheadle Heath and this became quite an important junction with several branches diverging from the main line, these being to Romiley, Stockport (Tiviot Dale) and Glazebrook. The main line then skirted the suburbs of Manchester, being joined by the Cheshire Lines Committee at Throstle Nest, before finally entering the magnificent Manchester Central terminus. This superb structure was in many respects almost as impressive as the Company's London terminus, St. Pancras. The semi-circular roof spanned a full 210 feet and was supported on sixteen steel arches which were in no way superfluous, for the huge canopy covered 1250,000 square feet! Unfortunately, having expended vast sums on the station roof, the Midland Company cut its spending when building the façade which was constructed of wood. It had originally been intended that this should be a purely temporary measure until sufficient funds became available to erect a more impressive feature, but, as things turned out, the money was never allotted and the wooden façade still survived in May 1969 when the station closed.

The Midland had now achieved its ambition of possessing its own direct route from Derby to Manchester after a thirty-one-year battle against both human and natural obstacles. The terrain through which the railway was driven was difficult by any standards and the problems which faced the engineers who built it were far greater than the usual impediments facing railway builders even in mountainous country. The profusion of tunnels and viaducts together with the fact that it was necessary to take the line over a summit almost 1,000 feet high all serve to emphasize this. But it was well worth the effort and expenditure for the Midland Railway could now run expresses from St. Pancras to Manchester over one of the finest main lines in the country. They had built a railway which was as magnificent as the beautiful scenery through which it passed.

3. The Scenic Qualities of the Route

The Peak Line was renowned for its great beauty and has been deservedly described by many as one of Britain's most scenic railways. It was a magnificent line with its great viaducts, tunnels, superb vistas and beautiful rolling countryside. Upland areas of the route were characterised by wild windswept moorland and quiet secluded dales. During the winter months the harsh weather conditions prevailing in the region produced a bleak white landscape possessing a stark beauty and charm of a totally different nature. Before the railway was built many considered that this area with its crags and chasms, crumbling limestone and rugged gritstone ridges was inaccessible. The railway followed the course of several river valleys including those of the Derwent and Wye, and towards the north the line was flanked by a number of very impressive peaks. Furthermore, to add to this natural splendour, the route ran through country known as 'the Dukeries', possessing famous oaks and magnificent stretches of unspoilt parkland.

From Derby heading northwards, the railway follows the course of the River Derwent to Ambergate, situated at the confluence of the Derwent and the River Amber. Here the present station of 1876, well known for its unusual triangular configuration and wooden platforms, hangs precariously over the A610 road from Ambergate to Ripley! Continuing north-westwards through the narrow Derwent Valley, the scenery to be observed from the railway becomes increasingly picturesque with the river and the Cromford Canal occupying the same dale, the sides of which are heavily wooded. The western slopes of the valley are occupied by Shining Cliff Wood and part of Alderwasley Park, while to the east of the line the small settlement of Crich, famed for its excellent working tramway museum, occupies the land above Crich Chase. An interesting memorial to the famous Sherwood Foresters Regiment, known as Crich Stand, which is sited on Crich Hill in a position where it overlooks the Regiment's recruiting counties of Derby and Nottingham, can also be seen. The railway then passes through the village of Whatstandwell before crossing the Derwent and conveniently bringing into view Lea Hurst, formerly the home of Florence Nightingale.

Travelling north-westwards to High Peak Junction, the route of the unfortunately defunct Cromford & High Peak Railway, which claimed the steepest conventionally worked gradient of any railway in this country, namely the 1 in 14 to Hopton Top, can be seen heading westwards on the path of its former steeply graded route to the still surviving Peak Forest Canal at Whaley Bridge. At Cromford on the main line, the station was built in a particularly attractive and unusual French style and is believed to have been designed by G. H. Stokes, the son-in-law of the famous 19th century architect Sir Joseph

Paxton, who was himself responsible for designing a number of stations on the Midland route to Manchester. To the west of the railway at Cromford is Willersley Castle whose occupants once included none other than James Arkwright, inventor of 'The Spinning Jenny'.

Matlock is the next centre of significance on the journey north, a well-known spa town that is still renowned for the very impressive, even spectacular, scenery which surrounds it. Matlock is divided into several districts including Matlock Bath and Matlock Bridge, both of which had stations serving them. Matlock Bath Station, the first to be reached when approaching from the south, was built in the style of a Swiss chalet no doubt in order that it should blend in with the image of the locality where one of the well-known features is actually called 'Switzerland View'. The small Matlock towns are rich in history and retain a wealth of possessions from the past, including ancient lead mines dating back to the Roman period and many other relics from by-gone ages. One of the most notable features is the Victorian Prospect Tower on the Heights of Abraham which were so named after the Battle of Quebec in 1759 where Wolfe was killed, the geography of the terrain being likened to the Canadian plateau on which the battle was fought. Natural features include High Tor, an impressive inland cliff which rises a sheer four hundred feet from the River Derwent. Beyond is Riber Castle, not a medieval fortification, but a Victorian folly built in 1862 by John Smedley, a local textile manufacturer. Unfortunately, this interesting structure fell into decay during the post-war years but the castle grounds now form the home of Riber Zoo. John Smedley was also largely responsible for the creation of the spa at Matlock Bank in 1852, the curative waters of this locality having, in fact, been known as far back as the 17th century.

The sections of the line between Matlock Bath and Matlock Bridge which actually see daylight are quite attractive, although it is unfortunate that a good part of this stretch of railway should be enclosed by the High Tor Tunnels which pierce the spurs of limestone along this part of the Derwent Valley. Matlock Bridge Station, now the Peak Railway Society Headquarters, was designed by Sir Joseph Paxton. Apparently the crime rate in the mid-19th century was as much of a problem then as it is today since the lead was completely stripped from the station roof the morning it was opened to traffic! Almost immediately after leaving Matlock Bridge on the route to Manchester, the sizeable Cawdor Quarries can be observed to the left of the main line which then proceeds onwards to the interesting settlement of Darley Dale. Here the features include Oaken Hill which is believed to be of volcanic origin, hopefully long extinct. This was once used as a site for the Roman fort of Occursus. Within the churchyard at Darley Dale there still exists a yew tree which is thought to be at least 2,000 years old, while in the church itself Burne-Jones's 'Song of Solomon' can be observed. The railway station at Darley Dale is an impressive Gothic structure which is fortunately still standing.

Continuing in the direction of Rowsley, the vast derelict site of the former extensive Rowsley Marshalling Yards can be seen. Hopefully at least a proportion of the land formerly occupied by the yards will be developed for the Peak Railway Project. The original station at Rowsley, built in 1849, which was later replaced by the building sited on the route of the Midland main line, still exists despite the fact that it ceased to be used as a railway station after the Midland decided to follow the new course to Manchester in the 1860s. The Midland station, which lacks some of the character of Paxton's old M.B.M. & M.J.R. structure, is of a more functional design but also remains standing. In the village square at Rowsley can be found a manor house dating from 1672 which has been converted into the attractive 'Peacock Hotel'. Beyond Rowsley the railway was taken beneath the grounds of Haddon Hall, a superb building situated on a limestone escarpment overlooking the Wye Valley, whose many interesting features include its representations of many forms of architecture of English design from the Norman to Georgian periods.

Continuing northwards in the direction of Buxton, the scenery becomes increasingly more impressive. The railway, sited one hundred feet above the floor of the Wye Valley after leaving Haddon Tunnel, provides an excellent vantage point for observing the beauty of the landscape. The line enters Bakewell, often referred to as the 'Capital of the Peak'. This is a town full of history and is the home of the famous Bakewell Puddings. The 'Rutland Arms', from where these creations originated, is still to be seen. The railway then continues its path along the Wye Valley past the stations of Hassop and Great Longstone, built to serve the stately homes, Chatsworth and Thornbridge Hall.

The glorious panorama of Monsal Dale becomes the next focus of attention as the railway crosses the magnificent viaduct over the River Wye. As Ruskin said, 'There was a rocky valley between Buxton and Bakewell once upon a time divine as the Vale of Tempe; you might have seen the gods there morning and evening—Apollo and all the sweet muses of light—walking in fair procession on the lawns of it, and to and fro among the pinnacles of its crags.'

Monsal Dale possesses a number of non-natural features which are worthy of note including the extensive earthworks of an Iron Age hillfort sited on the summit of Fin Cop, and the ruined Sheldon Mill which still contains two large iron water wheels. It is interesting to relate that the impressive Midland viaduct, which is itself nearly one hundred feet high, was nearly overshadowed by an even mightier structure contemplated by the Lancashire, Derbyshire and East Coast Railway Company which was intended to soar across the Wye Valley and the existing viaduct as well, at a height of three hundred feet which would have rendered it the tallest in the country. However, the L.D. & E.C.R. did not see all its aims fulfilled and the monster viaduct was one such project which never became a reality.

The main line to Manchester continues through Litton Dale, a beautiful piece of scenery which is almost inaccessible by road or on foot. A superb view

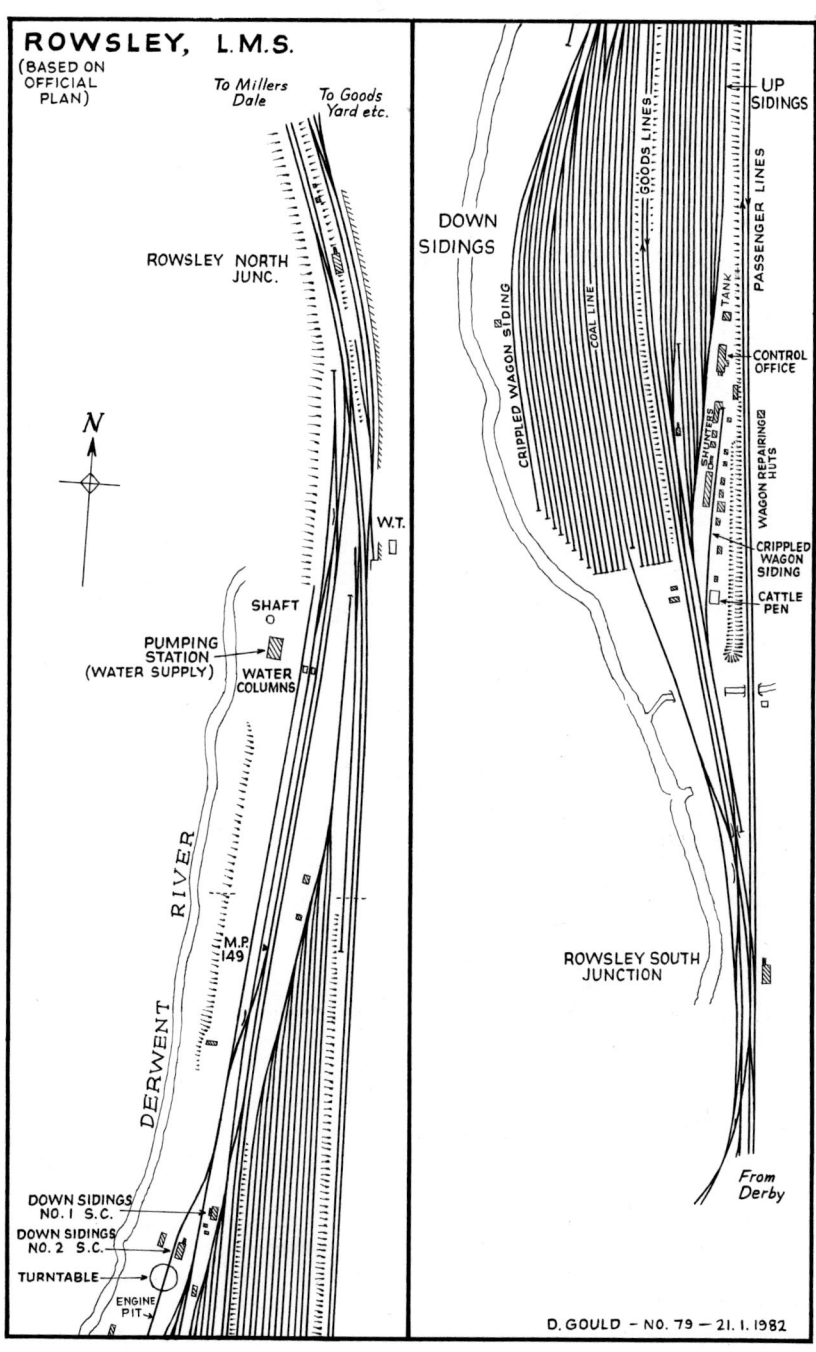

ROWSLEY, L.M.S.
(BASED ON OFFICIAL PLAN)

To Millers Dale

To Goods Yard etc.

ROWSLEY NORTH JUNC.

N

W.T.

SHAFT

PUMPING STATION (WATER SUPPLY)

WATER COLUMNS

DERWENT RIVER

M.P. 149

DOWN SIDINGS NO. 1 S.C.

DOWN SIDINGS NO. 2 S.C.

TURNTABLE

ENGINE PIT

DOWN SIDINGS

CRIPPLED WAGON SIDING

COAL LINE

GOODS LINES

TANK

SHUNTERS

PASSENGER LINES

UP SIDINGS

CONTROL OFFICE

WAGON REPAIRING HUTS

CRIPPLED WAGON SIDING

CATTLE PEN

ROWSLEY SOUTH JUNCTION

From Derby

D. GOULD – NO. 79 – 21.1.1982

of the River Wye can be observed from the stone embankment between Cressbrook and Litton Tunnels. The once quite impressive station at Millers Dale is then reached. This was formerly known as 'Millers Dale for Tideswell', since it served the local community as well as the many tourists and ramblers who visited this locality. At Millers Dale the railway crosses the B6049 road and the River Wye on two very impressive viaducts. The landscape here has been affected by quarrying but the wild and relatively natural appearance of the gorge has been maintained. Among the Dale's interesting features is a water mill which is still used for grinding corn. As the line proceeds westwards it passes under Chee Tor where the cliffs tower a full three hundred feet above the valley floor. At Millers Dale Junction the Buxton branch diverges from the main line and passes through Ashwood Dale where it jostles with the road and the river in the narrow confines of the valley. Buxton, situated at the end of the branch, is an attractive spa town which possesses many fine buildings dating from the Georgian and Victorian eras. Of these, the well-known Crescent, designed by John Carr of York in 1780, takes pride of place. Other buildings, including the thermal baths, were designed by Sir Joseph Paxton who appears to have been particularly active in this part of Derbyshire. Additional features of specific interest include the Pump Room, of Victorian classical architecture, and Solomon's Temple, a folly tower dating from 1896. There is also the Devonshire Hospital with its huge and distinctive dome. Until recently the former Midland Station could have been included here, but, as stated earlier, this fine structure was demolished some years ago.

Returning to the course of the main line, the scenery is ruggedly impressive as the railway passes through Great Rocks Dale on its way up to Peak Forest Summit. One striking feature here is the huge quarry to the left of the line, whose face, no less than four miles in length, has the distinction of being the largest in the country. Having cleared the summit the railway then descends through a deep limestone cutting to the notorious Dove Holes Tunnel and emerges a short distance south of Chapel-en-le-Frith. The countryside in this locality is particularly attractive and was formerly occupied by a famous deer forest belonging to the Crown. The town itself also possesses many reminders of by-gone ages, such as the curfew which still rings to this day. The church of St. Thomas à Becket dates from the early 13th century and was constructed by the keepers of the forest. The railway then continues to the isolated settlement of Chinley which is situated among wild but impressive moorland scenery. Features such as Chinley Churn and Combs Edge dominate the landscape of this area. Proceeding westwards to Buxworth the line passes through the deep cutting which marks the site of the former Buxworth Tunnel. As Manchester draws nearer the attractive Goyt Valley is reached, this being an important natural history preserve which was formerly covered by extensive woodland. However, the oaks and birches have now tended to give way to the rugged moorland scenery which dominates the Derbyshire Peak District. Beyond the Goyt Valley this type of landscape is replaced by undulating lowlands which are themselves superseded by the urban and industrial scene as the goal of the City is finally attained. There cannot be many railways in this country which traverse an area as rich in beauty and history as Derbyshire's Peak District.

GRADIENT PROFILE

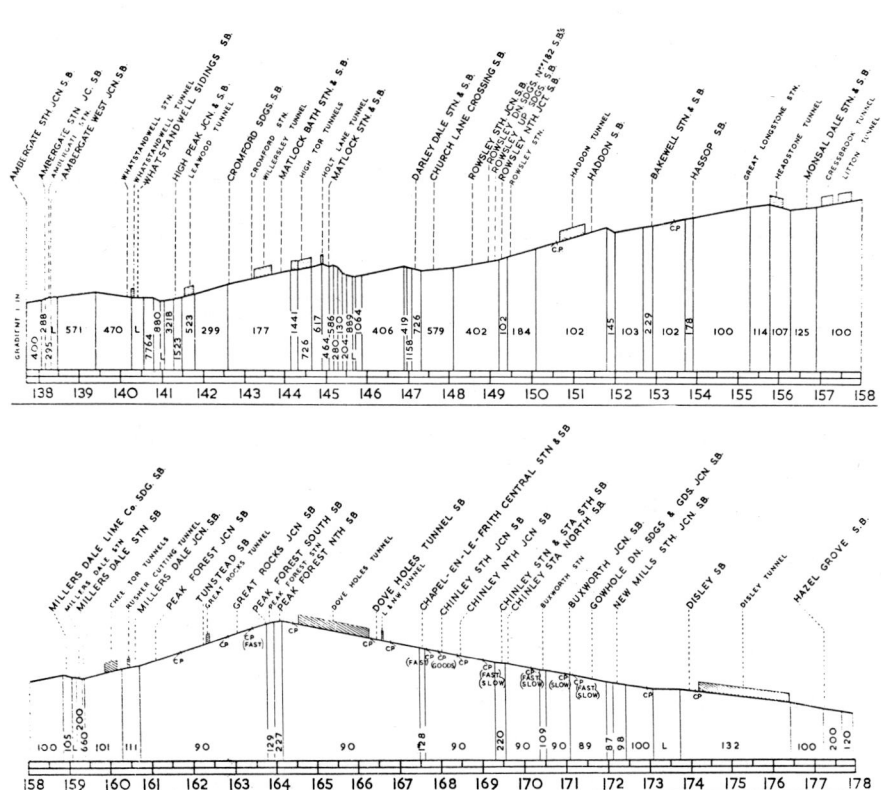

4. Operational History

During its century-long career as a major trunk route linking Derby with Manchester, the Peak Line could claim to be among the foremost lines in Britain. It was used by some of the most important express services including the famous 'Palatine', the 'Peak Express' and, in later years, the 'Midland Pullman' as well. During the Midland era the route was of great significance and handled a considerable quantity of both freight and passenger traffic. Following the 1923 Grouping traffic on the line was still increasing, as indeed it was on the British railway network generally. The 1920s witnessed the decline of the Lancashire coalfields, while new pits in Nottinghamshire and other parts of the East Midlands were being opened. Consequently there was a considerable increase in coal traffic over the Midland route to Manchester. Rowsley depot was upgraded and provided with banking locomotives for the purpose of assisting the increasingly lengthy trains over the steep gradients up to Peak Forest. Bankers were also provided at Gowhole freight yards to give assistance to Derby-bound trains.

It was in L.M.S. days that the gradual decline of the route began, partly as a result of the economic recession of the 1930s. Furthermore the rationalization of the railway network in 1923 had meant that many lines and facilities became superfluous. The closure of Buxton (Midland) locomotive depot during the L.M.S. period could perhaps be said to have been a foretaste of what was to come. The Second World War also had a damaging effect on the Midland route and the once fine pre-war St. Pancras–Manchester express services sank to a depressingly low ebb in the 1940s. The subsequent post-war recovery of the line came very slowly although passenger services were gradually brought back to their former high standards. However, yet another blow came in 1954 when it was discovered that the notorious Dove Holes Tunnel was unsound and following this unwelcome revelation it was decided that traffic should no longer pass through the tunnel at night. Obviously this was to prove a serious impediment to operations on the Ambergate–Chinley section and reduced its ability to compete with the rival ex-L.N.W.R. Euston–Manchester main line. During the period when the latter was subject to electrification work in the early 1960s, the Midland route enjoyed a last brief swansong, symbolised by the temporary use of its metals by the Midland Pullman service. However, this resurgence was of brief duration and once the electrification work on the 'West Coast' route had been completed that line became pre-eminent and with the insatiable demands for economies being made by British Railways at that time the days of the Peak Line were numbered. Gradually the 'through' traffic was either withdrawn or diverted and a general run down of the Midland route took place until the inevitable closure in the Spring of 1968, close to a hundred years after the Midland Railway had first run trains to Manchester.

Through services from St. Pancras to Manchester Central began in 1880 following the successful outcome of the Midland Railway's thirty-one year struggle to obtain its own route into Manchester. The Peak Line was now of considerable importance, being used by many 'inter city' expresses. During the following years Chinley grew to become an important junction, despite its remote location, and many expresses not to mention less significant services called here en route. Other local stations including Matlock, Bakewell and Millers Dale also had the privilege of being served by many trains which ran between Derby and the North-West. At Millers Dale, connections to and from Buxton were often provided and this helped to increase the former station's importance by no small degree. A typical example of a St. Pancras to Manchester service using the Ambergate–Chinley route in 1903 was the 10.15 a.m. (ex-St. Pancras) which departed from Derby at 1.12 p.m. and called at Ambergate, Matlock, Rowsley, Bakewell and Millers Dale. Here a connection for Buxton departed at 2.12 p.m. and arrived at the latter station ten minutes later. The main line service continued to Chinley and Manchester Central, and connections were made to Manchester Victoria and Liverpool.

Sleeping car services were operated by the Midland Railway over the Peak Forest route. In the summer of 1903 a sleeping car express left St. Pancras at 12.15 a.m. for Manchester Central and called at both Derby and Matlock Bath. It reached Manchester five hours after leaving London, at 5.15 a.m. The up-service from Manchester departed at 12.5 a.m. but did not stop at any stations on the Ambergate–Chinley section. Other services of interest which were run by the Midland at this time included a 'through' express to Blackpool which left Derby at 11.25 a.m. and called at Ambergate, Matlock and Bakewell. It did not stop at Millers Dale, no connection being provided to Buxton, but the service did call at Chinley and eventually reached Blackpool at 2.50 p.m. Not all the St. Pancras to Manchester expresses stopped at stations on the Ambergate–Chinley section of the Midland main line and some travelled via the Hope Valley line rather than the Peak Forest route. However, the Midland Railway timetable of 1903 did show that a number of London to Manchester trains including the 12.20 p.m. and 4.20 p.m. from St. Pancras did call at several stations on the Peak Line including Matlock, Rowsley and Bakewell in addition to Millers Dale where connections to Buxton were made.

Not surprisingly it was generally the local trains which served these somewhat isolated locations. In the early years of the century such services as the 7.13 a.m. and 9.45 a.m. from Derby stopped at all stations on the route to Buxton. Another departure from Derby was the 5.50 p.m. which ran to Bakewell, the twenty-five mile journey taking one hour and six minutes. There were some services which commenced from stations on the Peak Line, such as the 6.55 p.m. from Matlock Bath which, rather surprisingly, although it called at Rowsley and Bakewell, did not stop at the more important locations of Millers Dale or Chinley. This service ran to Manchester Central where it arrived at 8.22 p.m.

It is interesting to note how much time the Midland allowed for its trains when travelling between Derby and Manchester via Peak Forest summit. The 4.20 p.m. from St. Pancras to Manchester left Derby at 7.3 p.m. and was scheduled to cover the 53½ miles from there to Cheadle Heath in one hour and nine minutes. The 8.25 p.m. from Derby was allowed one hour and six minutes to travel the 41½ miles to Chinley although this included stops at Matlock, Bakewell and Millers Dale. In the opposite direction trains from Manchester were also given time to make the ascent up to Peak Forest. This side of the climb was often considered the more difficult, not only because of the lengthy gradients but because of the prevailing winds which tended to be worse when travelling from the Manchester direction and created discomfort and other problems for the locomotive crews particularly during the winter months. In 1903 the 4.40 p.m. from Manchester Central was given just over an hour to make the journey of about 30 miles to Buxton, this timing being typical for local trains on that route. Even the more important services such as the 7.45 p.m. from Manchester, which ran to St. Pancras, were allowed 55 minutes to reach Millers Dale. One must remember that the Midland Railway favoured a 'small engine policy' and had no locomotives larger than the Class 4 4-4-0 Compounds, so the climb to Peak Forest summit would have been a particularly gruelling and arduous one. Double-heading was very common on the Midland Railway and especially so over the Peak Line. It was not until the 1930s, when the L.M.S. had been in control for a decade or more, that larger passenger types such as Jubilees were drafted on to the St. Pancras–Manchester services.

Some of the services which travelled over the Peak Forest route from St. Pancras were bound for destinations beyond Manchester. The Midland timetable for the summer of 1903 showed a number of services bound for holiday locations such as Blackpool. In the opposite direction a train from Blackpool departed from Manchester Victoria at 12.5 p.m. and was allowed one hour and twenty-seven minutes to reach Derby including a two-minute stop at Millers Dale where connections were made with the branch service from Buxton. Most of the more important trains operated by the Midland over this line did not call at any of the stations on the Peak Line and the faster schedules were timed to make the journey to Derby in little more than an hour. With trains such as the 5.50 p.m. from Manchester Central, time was of the essence and the small Midland engines were given ample opportunity to show their paces. There is a quite well-known legend, which may have some foundation, concerning an incident which took place on the Peak Line at the beginning of the century. Some American tourists, boarding an express at Manchester Central, made loud adverse comments relating to the smallness of the Midland locomotive which was to head their train. They happened to be within earshot of the engine crew who were then determined to teach these 'colonials' a lesson. On the descent from Peak Forest they are reputed to have achieved a spectacular performance with the result that a considerable quantity of crockery in the dining car was smashed and passengers were ejected from their seats. Rowsley and Ambergate curves were said to have been taken at speeds never known before. An inspector awaited them at Derby and the crew were 'on the carpet' as a result of their transgressions. However, the legend has it that upon learning the full story the Midland authorities were so pleased that they had 'shown the flag' that pay was not stopped and the locomen were commended instead!

Fierce competition with the London and North Western Railway encouraged the Midland to make considerable improvements to its services to Manchester and Liverpool. A few months before the outbreak of World War 1 the Midland Railway opened its impressive Adelphi Hotel in Liverpool and consequently made efforts to attract custom. A new service was introduced which left St. Pancras at 6.10 p.m. and was timed to cover the 218 miles to Liverpool Central in four hours and ten minutes without any intermediate stops. The Midland also possessed high class hotels at St. Pancras and Manchester which provided incentives for encouraging patronage to the latter. The Company could offer many allurements to passengers in the form of high standards of comfort and an excellent dining car service which were well superior to those of the L.N.W.R. Both the rival routes from London to Manchester covered a similar distance but the Midland main line north of Derby, although it offered superb scenery, suffered from the problem of steep gradients. The L.N.W. main line, on the other hand, did not, with the result that the rival company was able to achieve faster schedules. The Midland route was also subject to speed restrictions which were often of great severity, such as those over the Ambergate curve and the Derby avoiding line. However, despite all these difficulties the Midland Railway could still achieve St. Pancras–Manchester timings of three hours and forty minutes which very nearly equalled the London and North Western's crack three and a half hour services.

This intense rivalry was brought to an end by the 1923 Grouping and the formation of the L.M.S. The initial result was a slight reduction in the level of services operating over the Midland route to Manchester. The L.M.S. period saw the disappearance of 'through' services to East and Mid-Lancashire and also the end of connections to Manchester from Bristol. However, services to Manchester Victoria continued and the Midland line was still of great importance. The 1927 L.M.S. timetables showed that there were many interesting services operating over the Peak Line at that time. These included a Continental Boat Express which was advertised as containing a through-carriage between Tilbury Marine and Manchester. The Down service from St. Pancras left Derby at 11.15 a.m. for Manchester Central and stopped at both Matlock and Millers Dale stations en route, although the Up service to St. Pancras did not stop at any locations on the Peak Line. This express was also advertised as containing 'through' carriages between Nottingham and Manchester. This service was the sort of working which makes modern 'block formations' of trains, which are not indelicate enough to give birth to through carriages, seem incredibly dull! The L.M.S. were very proud of their Boat Train, which was in competition with both the Southern and London and North Eastern Railways, and advertised it as the 'new route to France, Belgium, Switzerland and Italy (via Tilbury and Dunkerque)—Night Boat Service by the steamers of the Angleterre-Lorraine-Alsace S.S. Co . . .' Redundant ships (and staff—after 1928) were utilised from the L.M.S. fleet. Following closure of the Fleetwood–Belfast route in 1928 there were redundant officers and ratings from Fleetwood and Heysham who were sent to Tilbury. Unfortunately this service did not prove to be a success and was discontinued after a relatively short time span. In fact, the Midland Railway had also operated a Boat Train over the Peak Forest route. In 1910 the 2.30 p.m. down from St. Pancras (4.57 p.m. ex-Derby) included 'through' carriages from Deal, Dover and Folkestone to Manchester Central. No such schedule had existed at the turn of the century. St. Pancras–Manchester sleeping car services did run via the Peak Forest route at the beginning of the century but were no longer referred to in the 1910 Bradshaw nor in the L.M.S. timetables. During the L.M.S. Era the evening Down service (4.25 p.m., later the 4.30 p.m. ex-St. Pancras) was really a 'Boat Train', although it was not actually advertised as such, and ran to Liverpool. Unfortunately the post-war Nottingham–Liverpool services were not in the Boat Train category save during the summer when a connection was made with the Liverpool–Douglas sailings.

The 1927 L.M.S. timetables revealed that this period was one of the most interesting in the history of the line. Apart from the fact that there were Boat Trains running in both directions, many important services used the Peak route at this time. They included the 12.05 a.m. from St. Pancras to Manchester which left Derby at 3.55 a.m. and stopped at Matlock before continuing to Manchester Victoria and Liverpool. The 9.45 a.m. from Derby which called at several stations on the Peak Line including Matlock, Bakewell and Millers Dale, was advertised as containing a 'through' carriage from Nottingham to Manchester Victoria. The 10.25 a.m. ex-St. Pancras which left Derby at 1.08 p.m. incorporated a restaurant car and also a 'through' carriage to Liverpool. The 2.25 p.m. ex-St. Pancras which left Derby at 4.58 p.m. also contained a restaurant car and was advertised as including a 'through' carriage from London to Buxton. This train called at Millers Dale where the latter carriage was detached. The Sunday services in 1927 included a train from St. Pancras to Manchester which left Derby at 6.20 p.m. and called at a number of stations on the Peak Line including Matlock, Rowsley and Bakewell. In the Up' direction, Sunday departures at this period included the 9.15 a.m. ex-Manchester Central which stopped at Chinley and all stations on the Peak section excepting Monsal Dale and Hassop.

Local trains using the route in the late twenties included the 7.08 a.m. from Matlock which stopped at all stations to Millers Dale and then continued to

Chinley and Manchester Central. Both the 7.05 a.m. and 3.40 p.m. from Derby also stopped at every station on the Peak Line as far as Buxton.

A train from Liverpool and Manchester Central which left Chinley at 9.40 a.m. and called at Millers Dale where a carriage from Buxton was added contained a 'through' carriage from Liverpool to London and a restaurant car from Manchester. Derby was reached at 10.40 a.m. and St. Pancras at 1.30 p.m. Another train, which left Chinley at 10.39 a.m. and called at Millers Dale as well as Matlock, was advertised as including a 'through' carriage from Manchester Victoria to St. Pancras, and another departure which left Chinley at 2.22 p.m. contained 'through' carriages from Liverpool and Buxton to London. Local trains in the Up direction included departures such as the 6.03 a.m. and 2.0 p.m. from Manchester Central to Buxton. Services from Buxton included the 6.15 a.m. to Matlock which also stopped at Millers Dale, Bakewell and Rowsley. Other timings such as the 7.52 a.m. and 5.35 p.m. called at all stations from Buxton to Derby except Monsal Dale and Hassop. There were even some services which commenced from minor stations on the line, such as the 7.25 a.m. from Bakewell and the 1.37 p.m. from Darley Dale which ran to Derby.

During the period in the 1930s which has been described as the 'Second Golden Age of Railways', the L.M.S. made some quite substantial improvements to the standards and frequency of services over the line. In the later years of that decade the introduction of the new 'Jubilee' 4-6-0s to the Midland Division resulted in a fine renaissance in speed. The L.M.S. authorities decided that improving and accelerating the St. Pancras–Manchester services would bring considerable benefits to centres served by that Company such as Leicester and Derby. In addition the former L.N.W.R. 'West Coast Main Line' was now becoming overburdened with traffic and the revitalisation of the Midland route was a means whereby pressure on the former could be reduced. The L.M.S. timetables for 1937 showed that systematic departures for the Down expresses had been arranged and these were now leaving St. Pancras at twenty-five minutes past the hour. They were then known as the 'Twenty Fives' although this appellation became redundant in October of the same year when the starting times of these services were altered to thirty minutes past the hour. Thus, services which in 1927 had left St. Pancras at 10.25 a.m. 12.25 p.m. and 2.25 p.m. now left the terminus five minutes later. The newly re-timed 10.30 a.m. express was accelerated to make the run to Manchester in the fastest previous Midland route time of three hours and thirty-five minutes. This feat was all the more creditable since the train now had to make an additional stop, at Derby, and the length was increased to eight coaches. The Midland had not operated such heavy expresses over Peak Forest summit. In 1938 this service and the corresponding 4.25 p.m. Up were given the title of 'The Peak Express'. Similarly the 10.00 a.m. Up and the 4.30 p.m. Down became known as 'The Palatine'. The naming of these services emphasized the importance which the Peak Line had acquired. By 1939 the 10.30 a.m. 'Peak Express' was scheduled to stop at Matlock, Millers Dale and Chinley and reached Manchester Central at 2.26 p.m., just under four hours after leaving London. The equivalent service in 1937 had reached Manchester at 2.05 p.m., but the train made no intermediate stops at Derby. The Up 'Peak Express' made the journey to St. Pancras in three hours and forty-seven minutes, this timing being the same in 1939 as it had been two years earlier. The Down 'Palatine' contained a 'through' carriage from St. Pancras to Liverpool and made the journey to Manchester in the same time as the Down 'Peak Express' with stops at Matlock and Chinley as well as Derby. The Saturday service was slightly slower and did not reach Manchester Central until 8.39 p.m. thus taking more than four hours to make the journey. The Up 'Palatine' did not call at any stations on the Ambergate–Chinley section and was just one minute slower than the Up 'Peak Express', being timed to arrive in St. Pancras at 1.48 p.m. These schedules compared very favourably with those the Midland had been able to offer such as the 5.50 p.m. from Manchester Central which, in 1903, made the journey to London in four hours and ten minutes without calling at any stations on the Peak Line.

In many instances the services operated in 1939 were noticeably faster than the corresponding schedules of ten years earlier. For example, the 1.15 p.m. from Derby which in 1927 took almost three hours to reach Manchester was timed to make the same journey in only two hours and forty-seven minutes in 1939. During the late 'twenties the 2.25 p.m. express from St. Pancras which contained a 'through' carriage to Buxton was allowed four hours to cover the distance to Manchester. However, by 1939 the revised 2.30 p.m. service was expected to reach the city within a schedule which was tighter by a full twenty minutes. Many other timings had also been improved during the inter-war period such as the 2.30 p.m. from Liverpool which arrived at St. Pancras at 8.35 p.m. in 1927 but ten years later was booked to reach the same destination twenty-three minutes earlier. It was a great pity that the outbreak of war in September 1939 put an end to this expansion for the following six years, particularly when considering that this was really the beginning of the end for the Midland route to Manchester.

During World War 2 the services on the line sank to an appallingly low level from which they were in many cases never to recover. Three trains in both directions daily were undeservedly advertised as London-to-Manchester 'expresses' and vice versa, yet their journey times, which were as much as five hours and forty minutes or more would have been scorned by the Midland half a century earlier. The 'crack' services such as the 'Palatine' lost their recently acquired titles as a result of the stark regime of austerity which descended upon the country. This particular name was eventually revived in the late fifties but generally the fine pre-war schedules were not restored to their pre-eminence. The post-war resurrection of the 'Palatine' was rather half-hearted and the 'Peak Express' was not revived at all although the corresponding service continued to run in post-war years albeit without its former title.

Following the termination of hostilities, great efforts were made by the L.M.S. authorities to raise services out of the chaos into which they had fallen. The September 1946 timetable was a very ambitious one for the line with many trains being reinstated and schedules tightened once again. Expresses from London and Nottingham included services which left Derby at 8.06, 9.38 and 11.30 a.m., all of these calling at Matlock, Millers Dale and Chinley in the course of their journeys to Manchester. In the Up direction, expresses or semi-fasts included the 12.05 a.m. ex-Manchester Central which ran to Derby and St. Pancras. The 7.15 a.m. service stopped at Cheadle Heath, Millers Dale and Matlock before reaching Derby. It then continued to Loughborough, Leicester, Luton and St. Pancras. The 7.24 a.m. from Manchester called at all stations to Derby via Marple while the 9.00 a.m. train called at several locations including Millers Dale and Matlock during the course of its journey to London. The 10.00 a.m. ex-Manchester Central–St. Pancras contained a restaurant car, a welcome facility at this period. Afternoon services included trains such as the 4.34 p.m. which ran via Marple to Chinley and then called at Millers Dale, Bakewell and Matlock in the course of its run to Nottingham, part of which was over the Ambergate–Pye Bridge line. Schedules such as the 5.00 p.m. Down service non-stop from Derby were particularly ambitious for the immediate post-war period, although unfortunately they often had difficulty keeping time. In the Up direction, the 10.00 a.m. and 4.15 p.m. trains were of limited formation and on a Friday the latter is said to have been uncomfortably overcrowded. Both consisted of only seven bogies which usually comprised, from front to rear, a 1st Brake/Composite, 1st Corridor, 1st Open (Restaurant), Restaurant Car (Kitchen and 3rd Class), 3rd Open (×2) and Side Corridor (Brake Composite Third).

However, the severe fuel crisis and other troubles during the winter of 1947 greatly affected this new revitalised timetable and stifled progress once again. In the Down direction an early victim was the 5.08 p.m. to Buxton whose cancellation resulted in an outcry in the 'Derby Evening Telegraph' which was not assuaged by the 5.00 p.m. service commencing to call at Matlock, Millers Dale, Chinley and Cheadle Heath. Further cancellations followed, such as the 7.05 p.m. schedule, while in the Up direction the 10.00 p.m. train was also axed. It was well into the 1950s before a train approximating to this one appeared again, this being the 10.25 a.m. which called at Chinley, Millers Dale and Matlock. It did not have a restaurant car. By Easter some of the withdrawn trains had been reinstated and the Summer Timetable saw the restoration of the 7.05 p.m. from Derby along with the restaurant car. Unfortunately, the 5.00 p.m. schedule was never to become non-stop again. The Ambergate–Pye Bridge line lost its passenger service and this meant that in the Up direction the 4.34 p.m. ex-Manchester Central for Nottingham had to run to Derby and then forward to Nottingham. Efforts were still being made to improve the schedules of trains traversing the Peak Forest route and in 1948 the 7.15 a.m. Up and 2.15 p.m. Down began to convey a restaurant car, while a year later the 'through' coach for Buxton was restored. It was conveyed by the 2.15 p.m. (subsequently 2.25 p.m.) Down service. Following nationalisation, a determined effort was made to improve connections with Liverpool from the East Midlands, for a time. In the 1948/49 Timetable, the 9.02 a.m. ex-Nottingham was advertised to run through from Manchester Central to Liverpool Central. In fact it took the place of the Cheshire Lines Committee 11.30 a.m. Up service from Manchester. The C.L.C. did little to promote the train and if it was more than a few minutes later they would dispatch an impromptu 11.30 a.m. service of their own. Later when the C.L.C. organisation disappeared, this practice stopped and a late arrival at Manchester did not mean that Liverpool passengers were punished further by being made to wait for the next 'half hour' interval departure. In the 1949/50 Timetable a buffet car was introduced from Nottingham to Liverpool. This was a well-patronised service which had no precise counterpart in L.M.S. days, although the same could not be said of the Return Working which was unimaginative and poorly patronised. This latter service, the 3.30 p.m. ex-Liverpool Central, was sometimes powered by a Sheffield (Great Central) B1 4-6-0 which had earlier brought in a Hull/Liverpool train which ran for a year or so via Godley Junction avoiding Manchester. The 3.30 p.m. service left Manchester at 4.34 p.m. and pursued a pedestrian course to Derby and Nottingham via Marple. In the 1950s the Return Working was altered to 2.30 p.m. ex-Liverpool and 3.25 p.m. ex-Manchester with the first stop at Chinley. In later years, as services over the line declined in quality, the buffet car was discontinued as were the 'through' coaches to Liverpool.

The difficult and even hazardous nature of the Peak Line did at least have the effect of making it an ideal testing ground for new or experimental locomotives and rolling stock. No doubt the operating authorities were of the opinion that if a particular engine could perform satisfactorily on this steeply graded route there would be little to worry about and it would have no trouble elsewhere! Consequently the line became a very interesting section of the railway system where unusual forms of motive power could often be seen. In Midland days, Cecil Paget's ill-fated and almost mythical 2-6-2 locomotive, no. 2299, made at least one foray through the Derbyshire Peak District, via Matlock and Chinley. During the 1948 Locomotive Exchanges which followed nationalisation, this line was one of several which were used during the evaluation of various locomotive types from the four constituent companies which were amalgamated to form British Railways. One of the most interesting 'foreign' examples which worked over the line during the course of these trials was the Southern Bulleid Pacific: 34005 'Barnstaple'. Her competitors from other regions comprised inferior breeds such as L.N.E.R. B1s and L.M.S. 'Black Fives', and consequently the Pacific, with her tractive effort of 31,050lb, was able to show her superiority and put up a creditable performance.

The L.M.S. pioneer main line diesel no. 10000 entered revenue earning service in January 1948 and found itself rostered to work services over the former Midland main line between Derby and St. Pancras with occasional forays over the Peak Line to Manchester. Her sister locomotive, no. 10001, appeared for the first time during the spring of that year, being scheduled to work the 12.05 p.m. Derby—St. Pancras, returning on the 4.15 p.m. Down throughout to Manchester Central and finally taking the 12.05 a.m. train back as far as Derby. The L.M.S. designed 'cross country' diesel electric locomotive of 800 h.p., no. 10800, which was introduced at this period, also found itself diagrammed to work over the Peak Line. She handled such services as the 7.20 a.m. from Derby and the 11.35 a.m. Up train from Manchester Central. Owing to her rather limited power she was unable to haul the heaviest schedules such as the 12.05 a.m. Up which, with its long rake of bogie vans, possessed a gross tonnage which would have given serious problems to a relatively small locomotive. Yet another of the early diesel prototypes which ran trials over this section was the 1600 h.p. Fell diesel mechanical locomotive, no. 10100, which worked similar timings to those of no. 10800, together with additional schedules such as the 7.05 p.m. from Derby to Manchester. Unfortunately the Fell diesel did not prove a success in service. During the L.M.S. regime, the unusual Ljungstrom locomotive, built by Beyer Peacock of Manchester but never officially accepted by the railway company, was tested in 1928 on regular goods services between Derby and London and occasionally made forays further north via Peak Forest. The Peak Line had a particularly interesting history as a trial ground and the proximity of Derby Works was a contributory factor here together with the testing nature of the line itself.

A wide range of more common forms of motive power could also be seen at work on the line and the variety of locomotive types tended to become more varied as the years passed. By the early fifties many modern classes were being introduced to the area and these augmented the earlier Midland and L.M.S. designs. An examination of the locomotive allocations at Buxton shed in the summer of 1950 reveal that there were thirteen classes represented with fifty-five engines in residence. None of the Riddles Standard designs had yet been introduced and it was to be a while before they appeared on the line with any regularity. However, Buxton's allocation included machines of Midland, L.N.W.R. and L.M.S. origin. There were still three Class 2P 4-4-0s, one of which, 40531, was a Johnson locomotive with driving wheels of 7 ft. 0½ in. and an example of a class which had been introduced in 1891 and later rebuilt by Henry Fowler. The two other 4-4-0s had been built after the Grouping and possessed driving wheels of 6 ft. 9 in. diameter together with a working pressure of 180 lb. which was 20 lb. higher than that of the original Midland locomotives. In the years until nationalisation the Midland and L.M.S. 4-4-0s had been the mainstay of passenger workings over the Peak Line but during the fifties their numbers rapidly diminished and all had been withdrawn by 1962, their duties being taken over by more modern L.M.S. and B.R. types.

DMUs also appeared on the local services in the late fifties thereby speeding the departure of the old Midland engines.

In the early fifties Buxton also housed a number of ex-L.M.S. Fowler 2-6-4Ts for local passenger work which had replaced most of the small Midland tanks although two of these remained 'on shed'. Two 'Crabs', 42942 and 42943, were also stabled there along with a sizeable contingent of Stanier 8F 2-8-0s, a type which continued to work in the area until the demise of both the Peak Line and steam operation in 1968. These large freight engines were supplemented by a number of Midland 0-6-0s of the 3F and 4F classes which had worked on the line for many years and indeed continued to do so until the 1960s despite the fact that the former had been introduced as long ago as 1885. The fact that Buxton shed had formerly been owned by the L.N.W.R was emphasized by the collection of locomotives of North Western origin which occupied the depot. These comprised a number of Bowen-Cooke G2 and G2a 0-8-0s for freight work and also two ancient 1P tank engines, 46616 and 58092, the latter being the last survivor of a class introduced by Francis Webb in 1877 and retained until 1952 for working the Cromford & High Peak Railway. The stud at Buxton at this time was completed by two Midland 1P 0-4-4Ts which worked the branch to Millers Dale. Their task was eventually taken over by diesel railcars.

Rowsley shed also contained a varied selection of motive power and provided locomotives for the Cromford & High Peak Line as well as banking engines to assist freight trains up the steeply graded main line to Peak Forest. During the summer of 1950 it housed a total of fifty machines from ten classes. Most of these locomotives were small, the largest being two 'crabs' and an L.M.S. 3-cylinder Compound, 41049, although this situation had changed considerably ten years later by which time the depot had received a quota of B.R. Standard types including several 9F 2-10-0s! However, in the early fifties most of Rowsley's stud consisted of old Midland freight engines such as the Johnson 2F 0-6-0s which dated from 1878. Along with the later Midland and L.M.S. 0-6-0s, these had been stabled at the depot for many years. The tank loco allocation comprised several L.M.S 'Jintys' which occupied much of their time shunting in Rowsley marshalling yards, together with a solitary Midland 1F 0-6-0T and four ex-North London Railway 0-6-0Ts. The latter included 58850 which was not withdrawn until September 1960, two years after the other members of the class had disappeared, despite the fact that it had been the prototype, having entered traffic in 1880. These four North London tanks had been transferred to Rowsley in the early 1930s for working the Cromford & High Peak Line and continued to serve there until the late fifties when J94 0-6-0STs were drafted to the depot. 58850 was more fortunate than its sisters for it escaped the cutter's torch and now resides on the Bluebell Railway in Sussex.

Other locomotive types which regularly worked over the Peak Line were stabled at locations far distant from the area. During the fifties, Britannia

Pacifics were introduced to the Midland Division and regularly hauled the 'Palatine' and other important expresses. Trafford Park depot at Manchester provided many of these fine machines which included 70015 'Apollo', 70017 'Arrow', 70021 'Morning Star' and 70044 'Earl Haig'. With the general post-war recovery, in the summer of 1957 there came the raising of the speed limit over the principal Midland main lines to an impressive 90 m.p.h. which enabled a fundamental reorganisation of the Midland Division timetable to take place. Royal Scots and Patriots appeared on expresses over the Peak route although these always tended to be rather rare north of Derby on the Midland main line. The more widespread use of such large locomotives enabled a tightening of schedules. The reinstated post-war 'Palatine' was in fact a new service which was timed to leave St. Pancras at 7.55 a.m. and reach Manchester Central three hours and fifty-three minutes after leaving London, at 11.48 a.m. It included six stops, these being at Luton, Wellingborough, Leicester, Derby, Matlock and Millers Dale, yet it still managed to make the journey to Manchester twelve minutes quicker than the rival 7.45 a.m. 'Lancastrian' which followed the West Coast Main Line from Euston. On the Midland line the corresponding Up service which also acquired the title of 'the Palatine' was the 2.25 p.m. from Manchester Central to St. Pancras. This called at Chinley, Millers Dale, Matlock, Derby and Leicester and then covered the remaining ninety-nine miles to London in 'even time'—ninety-nine minutes, arriving in St. Pancras at 6.15 p.m. These timings were all the more creditable in view of the heavier loads which were handled in the post-nationalisation era. Through locomotive workings between St. Pancras and Manchester became commonplace with the principal services despite the fact that the round trip was almost three hundred and eighty miles. During this period the Down 'Palatine' was one of the lighter 'XL Limit' trains comprising an eight coach load of two hundred and eighty tons tare, the Up service being of a similar composition as far as Derby where a compartment first was added. A faster train was the 2.25 p.m. ex-St. Pancras which reached Derby at 4.38 p.m. and then made the journey to Manchester in one hour and twenty-five minutes.

It was unfortunate that the pre-war 'Peak Express' title was not revived as the 'Palatine' had been. However, a service which corresponded to the former working still continued to depart from Manchester Central at 4.35 p.m. taking one hour and nineteen minutes to reach Derby, without any intermediate stops. The train continued to St. Pancras where it arrived at 8.35 p.m. Further improvements to the services on the Midland main line were made in the late fifties and early sixties, partly as a result of electrification work which was being undertaken at that time over the rival West Coast route from Euston. Unfortunately the completion of this task as far north as Manchester was to bring about the downfall of the Peak Line, but the operation did at least have the effect of causing a proportion of the Western Division traffic to be temporarily transferred to the Midland route. For this reason the Midland

Pullman, which in the normal course of events would probably have run between Euston and Manchester London Road from the date of its introduction, was initially put into service between St. Pancras and Manchester Central. The train began operations in 1959-60 and not only restored the pre-war position but raised completely new standards of luxury and speed. It was the first time since Midland days that Pullman services had run between St. Pancras and the North-West, although the Midland Railway had been the first company to introduce Pullman cars to Britain, in 1872. The new trains, which were composed of six coach sets, each had two power cars which provided a total of no less than 2,000 h.p. with the result that the Pullmans were able to achieve timings of a mile a minute. A noteworthy feature of these trains was that some of the uphill speeds required of them were as fast as those downhill. This was the case with the climb from Chinley to Peak Forest where the Pullmans were expected to cover 5.7 miles of 1 in 90 gradient in only six minutes at an average speed of 57 m.p.h. The Manchester Pullman had the distinction of being the fastest service ever to make the journey between that city and London up to that time, beating the pre-war timings of the Western Division. In the Up direction it left Manchester Central at 8.50 a.m. reaching St. Pancras at 12.03 p.m. after a journey lasting three hours and thirteen minutes. The Down Pullman left St. Pancras at 6.10 p.m. and arrived in Manchester Central Station at 9.21 p.m. having taken a mere three hours and eleven minutes to make the journey from London, a distance of no less than 189 miles. These Pullmans ran via the Midland main line until 1966 by which time the electrification work on the former L.N.W.R route had been completed as far north as Preston, the Pullman services being accordingly transferred to the Western Division.

By the late 'fifties the motive power working over the Peak Line was being rapidly modernised with the introduction of new B.R. steam and diesel classes. The latter included a certain number of the Brush 1,160 h.p. Type 2s introduced in 1958 as well as larger Sulzer Type 4s for express work. The influx of new blood to the steam fleet included two types of WD Austerities with both the 2-8-0s and J94 0-6-0STs being represented, the latter being drafted to Rowsley shed for working over the Cromford & High Peak Line to Middleton Top. At Buxton mpd in May 1961, the steam types were slightly fewer in number than ten years earlier and dieselisation was encroaching noticeably. Stanier 2-8-0s remained in abundance as did L.N.W. 7F 0-8-0s although these latter Bowen-Cooke engines had a relatively short time left to live. About half a dozen 3F and 4F 0-6-0s were still 'on shed' as were a trio of Fowler 2-6-4Ts. By this time there were only thirty-eight steam locomotives in residence as against the total of fifty-five machines stabled there in 1950. This is not to say that the depot itself was in decline in the early sixties since a number of diesels had found accommodation there, including several 350 h.p. shunters and some larger Brush Type 2s. The older Midland locomotives including the Class 2P 4-4-0s and the veteran tank engines had faded from the scene. However, the scene at Buxton was still to retain an element of variety for a few more years to come and other classes such as Ivatt '2' 2-6-0s were allocated there. Two of these moguls, 46465 and 46480, were eventually based there for a time for the purpose of working passenger trains between Sheffield and Chinley. During 1965 when large express locomotives were becoming increasingly rare on the B.R. network, including the ex-L.M.S. Jubilee 4-6-0s, one member of the class, 45705 'Seahorse' found herself stationed at Buxton for the purpose of working morning commuter services to Manchester and evening trains in the return direction. Yet Jubilees were not the last express passenger engines to use the Peak Line, that honour having gone to the Britannias, in particular 70013 'Oliver Cromwell', which hauled a number of Specials over the Midland main line north of Derby during the summer of 1968 to mark the end of that route.

At Rowsley the situation was also fluid, with many new types of locomotive being allocated to the depot during its final years. During the summer of 1961 a total of 48 engines resided there, almost as many as had done so ten years earlier. Furthermore the motive power 'on shed' at this depot during the 1960s was of a far more modern nature than had been the case in the immediate post-nationalisation period. As at Buxton, the 4-4-0s had been retired by this time and the North London tanks had also gone. Fowler 0-6-0s formed the largest proportion of the stud, as they had done in L.M.S. days. They were backed up by a handful of Stanier 2-8-0s together with one or two of the remaining Midland 3F 0-6-0s. However, Rowsley had acquired far more dramatic motive power in the form of half a dozen B.R. Standard 9F 2-10-0s, a surprising fact considering that a few years earlier most of the engines at that depot had been small 0-6-0s and shunting tanks! In this way Rowsley shed enjoyed a last blaze of glory before its closure. In addition to the 9Fs a number of B.R. Standard '5' Caprottis were allocated there in later years together with two or three Fowler 2-6-4Ts for general duties. The tank engine stud in the sixties still consisted of L.M.S. 'Jintys' which had shunted Rowsley marshallng yards for many years, assisted by a small number of Austerity 0-6-0STs which helped out with this task in addition to their duties on the Cromford & High Peak Line. A solitary L.M.S. 0F shunter also remained there for the purpose of working between Sheep Pasture and Middleton. The majority of the old Midland engines which had formerly been allocated to Rowsley for many years had been retired by 1961, none of the Johnson 2F 0-6-0s remaining there by that time nor any 4-4-0s. Examples of the latter had lain derelict at the shed until 1959 but vintage locomotives were now becoming very scarce as the tide of modernisation and dieselisation swept such gems from the railway scene.

Despite the introduction of new steam and diesel classes together with the revitalisation of express services like the 'Palatine', the future of the Peak Line was placed in increasing doubt during the sixties. Regrettably most of the lines in the Peak District were unprofitable and would soon be condemned. The Beeching proposals and those which followed had a devastating effect and the harsh new policies were soon given practical implementation. After freight services ceased to travel via the Peak Line from March 1967 it was to be only another year until the complete demise of the route following the withdrawal of first the local passenger traffic and finally the eight daily expresses to and from Manchester plus their Sunday counterparts. The 'Palatine' was not to run again and the chance of reinstating the 'Peak Forest Express' was gone for good. Opportunities of bringing about a return to the halcyon days of the late 1930s, which were themselves sadly terminated at a time when it had appeared that there would be no end to the improvements in the quality of services, were thus never to be taken.

GRADIENT PROFILE

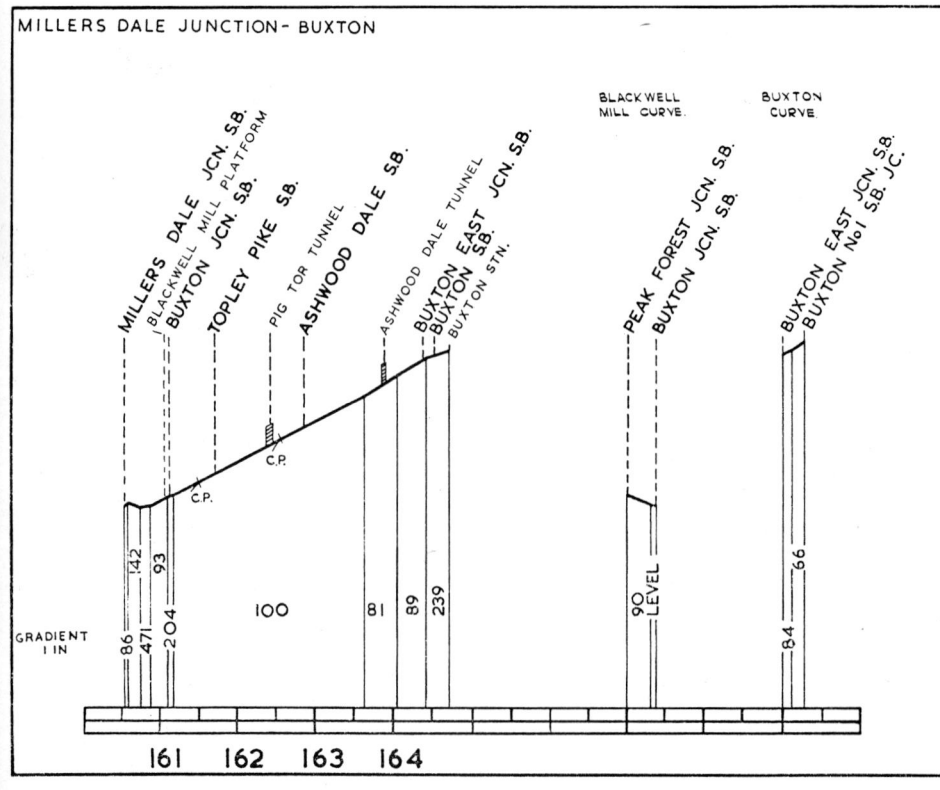

MILLERS DALE JUNCTION - BUXTON

5. Personal Reflections on the Peak Line

A history of the Peak Line would appear incomplete if it did not contain any personal impressions or narrations of the experiences of a few people who had close ties with it in their daily lives, either in the course of their employment as railwaymen or as passengers or interested observers. Despite the closure of much of the Ambergate – Chinley section and the truncation of the main line, many people still possess fond and vivid memories of the 'Manchester Bank' in its heyday. For engine crews the Peak Line was in many ways a difficult route to work in either direction, particularly in adverse weather, and often demanded considerable feats of skill from them. It is no easy task to restart a 400-ton train of limestone hoppers on a rising 1 in 90 gradient with a wet rail and an unhealthy locomotive. Travelling down grade there could also be problems of a different nature, particularly those involved with bringing a heavy unfitted freight from 45 m.p.h. to a stand on the almost continuous falling gradient from Peak Forest to Rowsley and beyond.

From the point of view of the interested passenger and bystander these problems were all for the professionals, the Peak Line being a magnificent railway which offered spectacular scenery in addition to its wealth of locomotives and the range of services which travelled over it. From the Midland era through to post-nationalisation days there was always something to be seen to provide interest, from the Compounds and 'Spinners' of the pre-Grouping years to the Scots, 9Fs and Britannias during the 1950s and 60s. For many people who knew the line well, its closure was a great loss for although it may have been unloved by faceless bureaucracy there was no lack of sentiment from those for whom the Peak Line was part of their lives.

One 'Man of the Footplate' with many a tale to tell of the Derby to Manchester run is Phil Higgins, a retired loco driver with fifty-one years of service on the railways. His allegiance is primarily with the London and North Western, a fact which is not surprising considering that he spent many years working from L.N.W. sheds, his first posting being to Llandudno Junction in 1923. During the hard years of the 1930s promotion was difficult to find and he decided, after attending Manchester College of Technology and other specialist academic institutions, to seek greater heights by transferring to the Midland Division of the L.M.S. In 1938 he became a senior fireman at Derby, a position he was to hold for only three years, for during the dark days of 1941, when the fortunes of the nation had reached their nadir, Phil's luck remained with him and he was promoted to driver. His career did not terminate until he retired from active service in November 1973. For twenty years he was an active member of the Editorial Board of the publication 'Locomotive Express', where his colleagues included such famous characters as Norman

McKillop, better known to many a schoolboy during the 1930s and 40s by his pen-name, 'Toram Beg'. Thus, Phil had ample opportunity, then as now, to write about his life as a locoman.

As Phil states, 'The Peak Line of the old Midland Railway provided some hair-raising experiences, unknown to the passengers thank goodness! A notable incident took place many years ago when I was firing a Patriot, a class of locomotive known to us then as the "Baby Scots" because of their similarity to their larger brethren. We were working an express for Derby and London and had made a fine turn of speed on the long descent from Peak Forest, roaring out of Headstones Tunnel, a somewhat appropriately named structure it would appear, and on to Monsal Dale viaduct at 75 m.p.h. At that time, some repair work had been undertaken to the structure but the workmen had built the wall of the parapet too high and had left some loose stones lying on top. Some of these were protruding rather too far in the direction of the permanent way and as we sped round the gentle curve over the viaduct, the front buffer beam of the Patriot struck the offending masonry a mighty blow sending it cascading down into the tranquil waters of the River Wye. Whether there happened to be anyone standing underneath I do not know, but if there had been they would certainly have received a message from the sky! My driver was watching for his distant signal at the time and I could not say whether he saw what happened for neither of us made any mention of this rather alarming incident, either to each other or to the operating authorities at the end of the journey. Our locomotive was simply reported later as having been found in the shed with a damaged buffer beam.

'However, the most harrowing experience I ever encountered on the Peak Line occurred during the very severe winter of 1947 which badly disrupted communications throughout the country, the Peak District naturally being hit far harder than the lowland areas. I remember that we struggled to work through a raging blizzard from our homes in Derby on this freezing Saturday night. My mate and I arrived at Derby No. 4 shed to sign on for the 9.15 p.m. "Mail" ex-Bristol. We were to prepare our own engine and take her out to relieve the Bristol locomotive from its train when it arrived at number one platform.

'Our engine was a magnificent Patriot, fresh from overhaul and painted in "Midland Lake" livery. As was usual with Derby Shop's turnouts, she was coupled to a Midland high-sided tender similar to those fitted to the Compounds. She looked beautiful, glistening in the reflected lights of Derby motive power depot. Preparation completed under extreme difficulties with snow blowing in and under every nook and cranny, we eventually managed to manoeuvre her under the hopper to take on upwards of six tons of coal. We then took the "engine line" from Derby shed, proceeding beyond Station North then back over the crossovers to the bay line. The "Bristol" arrived about eleven minutes late but since it was allowed thirty-eight minutes at Derby for traffic purposes from normal arrival time this lateness made little difference.

The station nameboard betrays the location of ex-LMS Class 5 4-6-0 45034 (John Robinson)

A panoramic view of Millers Dale with a banked freight heading towards Peak Forest Summit (J.H. Hatherley)

Ex-LNWR 2-4-0T No. 6422 at Buxton shed, July 1933 (R.W. Kidner)

Ex-LMS 4F 0-6-0 No.44169 standing at Buxton Midland station with a passenger train in June 1965 (Derek Cross)

B.R. Britannia 4-6-2 70042 'Lord Roberts' stands at Chinley Station with 'The Palatine', while an Ivatt Class 2 2-6-0 waits in the background (D. Larkin Collection)

A very battered Jubilee 4-6-0. 45598 'Basutoland' stands dumped in a siding at Chinley Station following a collision (M.L. Knighton)

Type 4 diesel, D56 'The Bedfordshire and Hertfordshire Regiment (T.A.) is seen here passing through Great Rocks Dale with a Manchester—Nottingham train on 11th. May 1967 (Derek Cross)

Ex-LMS 4F 0-6-0, 44167 reposes while her older ex-Midland sister 43967 storms over the bridge in impressive style (Derek Cross)

A Jubilee 4-6-0 is seen in this photograph in the deep cutting on the approaches to Dove Holes Tunnel [Derek Cross].

The unsuccessful prototype Fell diesel-mechanical locomotive 10 100 at Chapel-en-le-Frith station (D. Larkin Collection)

B.R. Britannia 4-6-2 70032 'Tennyson' hauls an express for Derby past an old ex-Midland 3F 0-6-0 (D. Larkin Collection)

Ex-LNER B1 4-6-0 61158 takes the New Mills avoiding line at New Mills South Junction (D. Larkin Collection)

Two 'Black Fives' stand in frozen but nevertheless attractive surroundings while "on shed" at Buxton (R.H. Griffiths)

The environs of Buxton Station are apparent as 'Seahorse' storms out of the station with a train for Manchester (Derek Cross)

Ex-LMS Jubilee 4-6-0 45705 'Seahorse' stands at Buxton Station on 18th. June 1965 (Derek Cross)

B.R. Type 4 'Peak' diesel D69 roars down grade past Buxton Junction with a train for Derby (Derek Cross)

Stanier 2-8-0 48168 rounds a rugged outcrop of limestone near Peak Forest Junction on 17th. 1965 (Derek Cross)

Type 4 'Peak' diesel D72 gets a clear road with a St. Pancras–Manchester express at Peak Forest Junction on 11th. June 1965 (Derek Cross)

Stanier 2-8-0   48442 hauls a southbound goods past the freight yards at Peak Forest on 12th. May 1967 (Derek Cross)

Stanier 2-8-0   48429 in scenic surroundings near Peak Forest Junction (Derek Cross)

An ex-LMS Stanier 8F 2-8-0 crosses the River Wye on the towering arches of Monsal Dale Viaduct (Peter J. Hughes)

An unidentified Britannia 4-6-2 is seen here after crossing Disley Viaduct with 'The Palatine'. (D. Larkin Collection)

Ex-LMS Jubilee 45705 'Seahorse' is seen again in the course of its journey at Peak Forest Station (Derek Cross)

Ex-LMS 2-6-4T 42610 stands at Peak Forest Station after a banking turn (Derek Cross)

Ex-GWR 4-6-0 4936 'Kinlet Hall' has been purchased by a consortium which includes the author, and is now resident on the Peak Railway (G.W. Sharpe Collection)

A panoramic view of Monsal Dale and the River Wye clearly illustrating the beauty of the scenery through which the Line passes (Copyright Locomotive 6201 Princess Elizabeth Locomotive Society Limited)

Ex-LMS Ivatt Class 2 2-6-0 46485, at that time employed on banking duties, stands at Peak Forest Station in company with Stanier 2-8-0: 48454 (Derek Cross)

Dove Holes station in 1970 (R.W. Kidner)

Stanier 2-8-0. 48519 tops Peak Forest Summit with a heavy limestone train (Derek Cross)

Ex-S.R. Rebuilt West Country 4-6-2 34101 'Hartland', purchased privately for eventual use on the Peak Railway, is unloaded at the premises of Shaw's Metals Ltd., Derby (Bob Lyle)

The BBC Blue Peter team filming restoration work in progress on ex-BR 4MT 2-6-4T 80080 at Matlock station in 1981 (R.A. Hunter)

Ex-LMS 8F 2-8-0 48624 undergoing restoration at Buxton. 9F 2-10-0 92214 can be seen in the background (R.A. Hunter)

With the train engine safely removed, we were signalled out of the bay and into the Down platform, our Patriot being much admired by passengers and station staff alike. Our train was made up to nine coaches, approximately 370 tons, and at the booked time of 9.15 p.m. we were given the "right away" and with gear set at 25% we glided out of No. 1 platform. Approaching Nottingham Road bridge, we entered our first "snow tunnel" which swept up and over the bridge, giving us a clear view of the signals ahead. We noticed the "distant" for St. Mary's set at caution and prepared for our first "stop" two miles out of Derby Station! Pulling up level with the signal box we received from the signalman our first warning of trouble ahead. We were told to reduce speed between there and Breadsall Crossing as the track was covered to an unknown depth and that platelayers were in attendance at points and crossovers! Creeping steadily under the road bridge we were confronted with a white blanket which had obliterated all signs of the permanent way.

'We eventually left Breadsall with an "all clear" as far as Duffield and my driver opened the regulator once again to first valve. Duffield was reached without any serious trouble and we dived into Milford tunnel with a sigh of relief, although we were dubious about the possible state of the exit. However, we gained confidence and accelerated to about 50 m.p.h. through Belper, the gear being set at 18% with the regulator at full first. At Broadholme we entered our second "snow tunnel", the tracks here being virtually free of snow as they are raised on an embankment about a hundred feet above ground level. My driver called across and asked me to spot the signals for Ambergate as he was unable to put his head round the cabside because of the ferocity of the gale. We took the left-hand curve over Anchor Bridge towards the sweep of Ambergate Station, our change of direction taking us head on into the snowstorm.

'We arrived at Matlock Station with about two feet of snow firmly embedded over the front buffer beam and a similar amount on the tender top and along the gangways of the coaches, giving us a streamlined appearance! The station staff were very helpful and removed some of this added weight while my driver and I prepared the locomotive for the difficult road ahead. We left Matlock a full one hour and twenty minutes late with a warning from the Station Inspector of trouble between there and Rowsley. It was at Darley Dale that we ran into our first snowdrift. We were doing about 40 m.p.h. when we were confronted with a white wall which very effectively barred our way. My driver shut off steam, applied the vacuum and we skidded to a halt amidst a cloud of frozen particles as our steed buried her nose in the snow.

'The only course of action was to dig our way out. I took my shovel and began to clear a path, the task not being quite as difficult as I had expected, for daylight appeared after about three yards of clearance. We resumed our journey, Darley Dale box giving us a free run to Rowsley where snowploughs from the depot had been active. We considered it strange that no traffic had passed us in the opposite direction. With full regulator we began to gain momentum comfortably, but crossing the Derwent Bridge where the track bends sharply to the left, our Patriot began to slip violently. The regulator was closed and the gear lowered to 28%, the sanders also being brought into use to assist adhesion. She overcame her "coughing bout" and reached 60 m.p.h. on the approach to Bakewell. Conditions became worse as we stormed up-grade into the Peak. At Monsal Dale we met our second blizzard which unfortunately blew in my side and made my life particularly unpleasant. At Millers Dale Station all the platforms were buried under several feet of snow, as was our Down line, but we managed to blast a path through the drifts without any great difficulty. However, our speed fell to around 30 m.p.h. despite the fact that our locomotive was keeping up the tradition of good steaming.

'From here onwards our troubles really began. On the approach to Chinley North Junction, the track skirted a cutting wall and here we were met by another mountain of snow completely blocking our path. We were only doing about 25 m.p.h. but the Patriot became firmly embedded in the twenty foot drift and made visible signs of her presence by "blowing off" sky high. We were stuck! Meanwhile the blizzard did all within its power to bury us completely. Our first task was self-preservation, and with a combined struggle against all odds, we managed to readjust the stormsheet to keep as much snow as possible away from the footplate. The snow was level with the footframe making it virtually impossible for us to leave the cab. We were also marooned. With the coming of dawn we could assess our position, the first thought being communication. I decided, with my driver's permission, to clamber over the coal to reach the first coach. With some help from the anxious passengers inside, I managed to gain entry and proceeded through the corridors to the guard's compartment. I met him half way along the train and together we tried to assure the passengers that everything was O.K. We needed to provide protection at the rear of the train so the guard ventured out to place detonators on the track, three-quarters of a mile behind the rear coach.

'By Sunday afternoon we were still alone in this desolate place. We were unable to leave the footplate now as the snow had accumulated to half way up the side of the boiler and the left-hand side of the train was completely buried. The only way out seemed to be via the guard's compartment so it was decided, while there was still daylight, to attempt to make an exit from the rear of the train, taking our implements together with two volunteers drawn from the ranks of the passengers. We managed to get out of the rear coach and started to dig a path towards the opposite bank and then in the direction of Chinley North Signal Box, which we eventually reached following two hours' hard labour, much to the relief of both ourselves and the signalman who had been trapped in his cabin since Saturday night!

'From the signal box we were able to observe the cab-top and upper boiler casing of our Patriot together with the outline of the higher parts of the tender and three coaches. No more of the train was visible as a result of the drifts. After making arrangements with the signalman for the delivery of food supplies to our beleaguered passengers, we attempted to dig our way back to the engine. We followed a straight line aimed at the tender, making the lucky find of a fire-cresset buried in several feet of snow in a platelayers' hut. We then made slow but steady progress, being rewarded some time later by the additional discovery of a tender axlebox lying beneath an eight-foot drift. We also found that it was firmly attached to a tender frame! I banged on the tank side with my shovel and was greeted by my anxious driver, George, who exclaimed, "What the hell's going on!"

'Thoroughly exhausted, we were greeted with rounds of toast and buckets of liquid refreshment. Our passengers were not forgotten, and the guard and our two volunteers took two firebuckets full of tea to their assistance. George and I retraced our "cutting" through the snow and dragged the cresset to the engine steps. The idea was to use it as a heater to prevent the tank-water freezing overnight. We shovelled snow into the tank from the cliff side until we were satisfied that it was reasonably full. The cresset was left to burn while I settled down to sleep. Early in the morning the guard came to the locomotive to inform us that the passengers were all comfortable and that everyone had been most helpful. Meanwhile George slept on soundly. The guard beckoned me down off the footplate and pointed out the fact that the fire-cresset was burning the brand new paint off the tender side, revealing the bare plates beneath! We pulled the cresset away and I wondered what my driver would say when he found out. We both returned to the cab and woke him. It was decided that we would attempt another journey to the signal box through our snow cutting. The news from the signal box was that help was near at hand and the rescuers had worked their way to a point only a mile from Chinley. It was with a sigh of relief and a shout from the passengers that we observed a cloud of steam and heard the familiar sound of another engine-beat and the blast of a whistle. George returned the greeting from our Patriot. We were rescued! The rescuers turned out to be troops who were soon in action, making short work of clearing the deep drifts around our train and distributing food and hot drinks to ourselves and our 119 passengers. Both George and myself were eventually relieved at about 2.30 a.m. and our engine was taken charge of by a second set of men from Rowsley shed. This was on the Tuesday morning, our ordeal having thus lasted nearly three days. At the rear of the train we found a light engine awaiting us together with a brake which had been provided to transport us back to Ambergate. From that location we were then given a lift back to Derby on the Up Sheffield parcels service.'

Two months later the driver, fireman and guard of the train were presented with an autographed scroll congratulating them on their efforts, a £5 cheque each, subscribed by the passengers, and a commendation on each record card!

Another man who possesses great admiration for the Peak Line is A. Derek Bryan, of Chesterfield, who, like many people, often used to travel many miles to see steam in action on the 'Manchester Bank'. He relates: 'My first recollection of the line was during the war years when I travelled on a special from Chesterfield to Buxton via the Ambergate triangle, hauled by a "Crab". This initial encounter with the Peak Line stimulated my interest in this stretch of railway and during the ensuing years right up to the closure of the Matlock – Millers Dale section, I spent many hours near Rowsley North Junction Signal Box watching the passage of trains on the main line, and the multifarious activities in the busy marshalling yard. In these sidings the shunting operations were undertaken by L.M.S. "Jinty" 0-6-0Ts and Stanier 2-8-0s. The occasional WD Austerity also put in an appearance here. The existence of the long gradient running north to Millers Dale and Peak Forest necessitated the provision of a number of banking engines at Rowsley shed, mainly 3F and 4F 0-6-0s and a few 2-6-4Ts which occupied their time assisting freight trains up to the summit. The Peak Line handled a healthy volume of traffic in its heyday and these relatively small locomotives had to work hard for their living. The ascent to Peak Forest, banking a long and heavy freight, would be a noisy business taking some time to accomplish owing to the considerable length and steepness of the climb. Having completed their tasks, the bank engines would then run back light over the Up main line and cross over into the yard area immediately south of the North Junction Box.

'In contrast to the bustle of the marshalling yards, Rowsley locomotive depot was a sylvan setting on Sunday evenings when a variety of engines reposed in the shed environs after the previous week's labours. Thick brown smoke would curl slowly and gracefully from their chimneys into the still evening air. An atmosphere of complete tranquillity pervaded this peaceful scene which was further enhanced by the attractive countryside which surrounded the depot and yards. Another of my favourite haunts in those days was the woodland path which ran by the lineside just to the south of Matlock. A particular delight was to observe the southbound "Palatine", a spectacle which I had the fortune to see on many occasions as it thundered down-grade towards Derby, almost always hauled by a Britannia. I have a treasured reproduction of a photograph of the Pacific, "William Shakespeare", seen in pristine condition at the 1951 "Festival of Britain" where this fine locomotive was exhibited. One can imagine my consternation, however, when I observed this same engine on an Up express, hauling its train past Rowsley North Junction Signal Box in an appallingly neglected and grimy state. Its smokebox was covered in rust as were numerous other parts of its anatomy and it was clear that no-one cared for this locomotive any more. For me this was a very tragic sight, but an all-too-common one during the closing years of steam. Patriots were not a particularly frequent sight on the Peak Line, but one evening when I was walking through Monsal Dale I was fortunate enough to see the rebuilt locomotive, "Prestatyn", dash past with a Sunday evening express for London.

'Recalling journeys over the line I can remember the thrill which I experienced when crossing Monsal Dale Viaduct and viewing the magnificent scenery. I had often stood in the bottom of the valley and admired the structure from there, but the scene appeared far more impressive when viewed from lofty heights above the Wye. A journey by train which, on other routes, would be rather mundane and uninspiring, was for me an experience to be long remembered whenever I travelled over the Peak Line. It had great character and charm, there being no other railway like it. There was not only the tranquil beauty of the landscape to be observed but also the works of man, some of them rather strange and bizarre. The line was noted for the eccentricity of its stationmasters, the gentleman at Millers Dale being no exception to the rule. As a result of his enthusiasm for entomology the station canopy became adorned with giant carved insects. I remember that the first time I travelled over the route, I was not unjustifiably alarmed to see enormous wasps and grasshoppers, reminiscent of mutations from a grotesque midnight horror movie, settled on the aesthetic wooden edging of the platform awnings!'

It is clear that although the greater part of the Peak Line was closed more than a decade ago, the character and charisma of this former trunk route continue to influence the lives of many people. Few individuals could serve as finer illustrations of this statement than John Gilberthorpe, who was so strongly influenced by experiences of the line during his formative years that he became determined to follow steam to the far corners of the globe following dieselisation in this country. Today he works for South African Railways and, in 1979, was promoted to driver at Germiston depot in the Transvaal where his steeds include giant Garratts and 4-8-4s, very different machines from the Midland 0-6-0s which he used to watch at Monsal Dale in his boyhood. Like Mr. Derek Bryan, he would travel many miles from his home in Sheffield for the purpose of watching steam in action on the Peak Forest route. As he himself explains: 'My first encounter with the Peak Line was in 1950 when I was just three years old. I had accompanied my parents to Monsal Dale and we enjoyed a summer afternoon by the tranquil waters of the River Wye. Suddenly my attention was captivated by a Stanier "hooter" and the roar of a train rushing at speed out of the tunnel and along the embankment. I waited impatiently, trying to peer over a dry-stone wall, and did not have to wait long before I was rewarded by the sight of a 4F 0-6-0, "waddling" from side to side with each piston thrust. I was terrified by this awesome spectacle, with the heavy beat of the locomotive rebounding and reverberating off the limestone rocks, magnifying the sound tenfold. I never lost my enthusiasm and from the age of 11 made journeys by bus to Bakewell with my friend, Graham Brookes. We would board the Sheffield Corporation single-decker early in the morning with thoughts of Britannias and Royal Scots filling our minds. One might ask why we did not patronise the rail service, but this was too infrequent and the journey would have been made much longer. On the Peak Line, stopping trains tended to be rare and we would have had to travel via Chinley or Ambergate, connections being few and far between. Bakewell Station was situated on the hillside, high above the town, and in order to reach it we would have to struggle up there in the growing heat of a summer day with our duffel bags strapped to our backs. We did not mind this labour, for the exhaust of a locomotive blasting up-grade from Rowsley would lend fleetness of foot! We followed a pretty lane which crossed the station on a Midland stone overbridge and from there we would gravitate to the golf course, situated to the south of the station, which offered an excellent vantage point for observing the passage of trains. Freight services were frequent and handled principally by Stanier 2-8-0s, 4F 0-6-0s and old Midland 3Fs which, possibly owing to their advancing age, always seemed to find the adverse grade a struggle to defeat. Crab 2-6-0s also made appearances on freights and most were banked from Rowsley. WD 2-8-0s also worked over the line, handling a proportion of the heavier mineral and goods traffic. It always gave me pleasure to watch the drivers skilfully at their posts and the firemen vigorously feeding the ever-hungry fireboxes on the long climb up to the summit.

'From the Derby direction, the exhausts of the train engine and then the banker would build up to a crescendo as they passed and seemed to take a considerable length of time to fade away as they curved round the hillside in a graceful arc in the direction of Hassop. By comparison, the descending freights were almost silent and gave little warning of their approach. I remember that 4F 0-6-0s of both the original Midland and later L.M.S. varieties could be seen at work in this locality. There were examples with both left- and right-hand drive and some had tender cabs which were without doubt a great advantage for locomotive crews during the severe Derbyshire winters. Fast passenger services were largely the preserve of ex-L.M.S class 5s and the Jubilees and one could always identify their approach from the Haddon direction by the much quicker beat of the locomotive. The Jubilees were particularly distinctive in this respect and could be recognised by the six beats from their 3 cylinders. They were never banked and rarely double-headed. These engines were usually from Trafford Park, Kentish Town or Derby sheds. I remember one memorable day when we were standing on the stone overbridge at Bakewell Station. We could hear the urgent six beats of a Jubilee climbing the bank and making a great effort. No. 45698 "Mars", a Bank Hall engine, shattered the peace of the slumbering station as the platforms shimmered in the heat haze, shaking the bridge and everything else as she stormed up-grade with her long rake of coaches. Locomotives from Bank Hall were rare on this line and the appearance of that particular Jubilee was an added bonus.

'Buxton Station was becoming of less importance by this period in time but locomotives which could be seen there included 2-6-4Ts, Class 5 4-6-0s and Crabs. Even as early as 1959, the passenger services which ran here had become subject to dieselisation and from that time onwards Metrovick Co-Bos and Sulzer Type 2s became increasingly frequent. In contrast, the 4-4-0s, which had been an everyday sight on the line for so long, were now hardly ever seen. This did not mean the end of steam operation over the Peak Line for it was to continue for some years. Jubilees were really the monarchs of the Peak Forest route and I can still remember them vividly, names such as "Leeward

Islands", "Malta G.C.", "New Brunswick", "Nyasaland" and "Jellicoe". Many of them passed through the Peak District on the occasions when Graham and I had the fortune to be watching at the lineside. However, some of the locomotives were very elusive from our viewpoint, the Kentish Town Jubilee, "Blake", being a particularly rare sight as were the later "457" variety named after warships.

'Later in the afternoon would come the day's big event, the approach of the "Palatine" travelling from Manchester to St. Pancras. It would roar down-grade with little warning save for the long chime whistle, a beautiful sound, echoing around the valley if the locomotive at the head of the train was a Britannia, and it almost invariably was. Most of these were from Trafford Park depot and regular performers on this train included 70042 "Lord Roberts", 70043 "Lord Kitchener" and 70044 "Earl Haig". There were others which appeared from time to time and on occasions a Royal Scot headed the express although these were decidedly rare on the Peak Line. Following the dramatic passage of the "Palatine", when our duffel bags were considerably lighter, we would walk along by the side of the fence which ran downhill towards the north end of Haddon Tunnel. I used to love watching the trains burst out of the portal. One would hear the muffled beat growing louder within the depths of the black abyss until suddenly the train would burst forth into daylight. A long chimneyed 3F 0-6-0 was always particularly interesting to watch on such occasions and if a banker was assisting at the rear, its crew would thrust their heads from the cab in order to get a much needed breath of fresh air immediately upon emerging into the sunlight. Our walk would continue past the extensive marshalling yards at Rowsley where there was always plenty of activity. It struck me as being rather strange to find a sizeable and busy yard set far away from civilisation in such beautiful surroundings beside the River Derwent. As I recall, the yards were mainly gas-lit with only a few electric lights in evidence. It all helped to add to the atmosphere of the place, as did the semaphores, standing like gaunt and silent sentries in the midst of the great expanse of trackwork and sidings. We continued our journey which followed the cinder path beside the Derwent to Rowsley locomotive sheds. We would scale the wooden fence and make a smart pace across a field to enter the depot from the rear to evade the shed foreman. He probably had a good laugh on occasions when seeing two frightened youngsters bolting like startled rabbits. However, we never aborted the expedition and as soon as we had decided that the coast was clear we would make a second attempt at gaining entry. Of the locomotives which resided in the depot, I remember that there were two old ex-Midland 2F 0-6-0s which had been "put out to grass" next to the stop-blocks at the end of the sidings. Another permanent resident during this period was the ex-North London 0-6-0T 58850 which we never saw used. Large numbers of 4F 0-6-0s were always much in evidence, many being in steam while some would be being washed out. The old Midland 3F 0-6-0s were also active, even into the early sixties.

'Following our investigations of the shed, we would usually saunter back through the marshalling yards, taking a final look at the varied sights to be seen at this unusual outpost of activity in the heart of the peaceful Derbyshire countryside. It would now be time to board the stopping train from Rowsley to Bakewell, often hauled by a 2-6-4T or a Crab. From there, we took the old single decker bus for the return home, crossing over the packhorse bridge at Bakewell and catching a last glimpse of the main line as we crossed the Midland overbridges. Sometimes, in the setting sun, yet another goods train, banked in the rear, would be curving its way high above the town, twin columns of smoke towering into the evening sky.

'Finally, one of my most treasured recollections, which I consider to be a fitting conclusion to my account of the Peak Line as I knew it, relates to the year 1965 when steam operation was being rapidly phased out. Most of the remaining steam locomotives were dirty, unkempt and in a generally run-down condition. This tragic situation overcame even the finest locomotives such as the majestic Jubilees, which had suffered severe decimation as a result of the onslaught of dieselisation. Yet with their numbers reduced to a relative handful, 45705 "Seahorse", was allocated to Buxton shed and became a familiar sight in the locality for some months proving that steam was still fighting for survival and was not beaten at this time. Every morning she worked the commuter train to Manchester and returned each day with the evening service. In contrast to the sorry and neglected state in which most locomotives found themselves by that stage in time, "Seahorse" was always turned out in immaculate condition and enthusiasts were reputed to clean her at weekends when the commuter trains were not running. One evening I saw her climbing out of Chapel-en-le-Frith into the sunset and tears came to my eyes as her glorious three-cylinder beat echoed from the hills and rays of sunlight danced on her gleaming paintwork. I hope that in time such sights will be seen again with the success of the preservation project.'

6. The Situation Today

The closure of much of the Ambergate–Chinley section did not mean the end for the Midland route to Manchester. Even today, B.R. passenger services still reach Matlock from Derby although the main line has now been reduced to single track along this section, the former trunk route being relegated to the status of a mere branch. Ironically, the years since closure of the main line have witnessed an increase in traffic over the sections which still survive. In the north, freight services run south to Peak Forest Junction and still traverse the Buxton branch to reach the adjacent quarries in Great Rocks and Ashwood Dales. When B.R. abandoned the route as a link connecting the two cities of Derby and Manchester they do not appear to have considered the potential of the Peak District region for generating traffic itself. The considerable number of tourists who visit the area every year could have provided sufficient revenue to merit the retention of the route if the services had been sufficiently orientated towards encouraging them to use this line.

Between Matlock and Peak Forest Junction, the demolition of the tracks and the removal of certain other features including the important bridge across the A6 main road at Rowsley have not seen the abandonment of interest in this section of railway. The proposal to rebuild the line has attracted considerable support on a national scale and this has enabled work to begin towards the long-term aim of the reinstatement of services between Matlock and Buxton. This is a very ambitious railway restoration scheme but it is unlikely that any of the obstacles to be faced in the process of reconstruction will be insurmountable in the long term. The task of relaying in excess of twenty miles of track will certainly be no small-scale operation either in terms of cost or of physical effort. However, the basic trackbed is still in sound condition and is unlikely to present the engineers with many difficulties.

Dealing with the section between Matlock and Rowsley, this 4½-mile length will probably be the easiest to rebuild although ironically, difficulties with planning permission and operational problems are likely to be greatest here. However, these obstacles are likely to be overcome in course of time. The station at Matlock is still used by B.R. who have retained one platform. The Peak Railway Society Ltd. and Peak Rail Operations Ltd. have already obtained a firm foothold here and Sunday passenger services to Derby, using chartered B.R. DMUs are now being operated by P.R.O. during the summer. The station yard now provides a home for two locomotives, one of them part-owned by the author, which are currently undergoing the long task of rebuilding so that they may eventually be seen at work again, in the attractive setting which the Peak Line offers. Heading northwards to Darley Dale, some of the track remains 'in situ' and at Darley Dale itself the station building is in remarkably good condition. Two miles farther north, Rowsley Station is reached together with the vast site of the former marshalling yards. Planning permission for development of part of this currently disused real estate has been obtained by Peak Rail Operations with the aim of creating a locomotive depot and maintenance facilities.

Between Rowsley and Great Longstone the most difficult civil engineering problems will be encountered and the replacement of the missing bridge over the A6 at Rowsley will probably present the greatest single physical obstacle in the path of the reinstatement of the line. Since the removal of this bridge, the road level of the A6 has been raised by more than a foot with the inconvenient result that before reconstruction of the bridge is possible, the trackbed will need to be banked on the southern side in order to allow sufficient clearance of the road. Fortunately, on the northern side there is an up gradient which will only require levelling in order to meet the new bridge height. From Rowsley, heading west, the next structure which could cause some headaches is Haddon Tunnel although this building has been found to be in better condition than had been expected. At Bakewell, the station building is now in the process of being restored and it will be pleasing to see this fine structure restored to its former glory. Between Bakewell and Great Longstone the line passes under and over a number of roads but fortunately, in all cases, the bridges appear sound. The two stations at Hassop and Great Longstone are currently occupied by private firms.

The remaining nine miles to Buxton contain those features which are usually most prominent in everyone's memory of the line. The section includes Monsal Dale Viaduct whose condition is reported as very good and there are not likely to be any undue problems encountered with either its repair or maintenance. Of Monsal Dale Station, only the northbound platform remains but the trackbed is still reassuringly sound. The same can be said of the two tunnels at Cressbrook and Litton which are both in a surprisingly good state of repair. Millers Dale Station is the next structure of significance, this being quite a large building with several platforms. A considerable amount of money and physical effort will be required to restore the buildings to their original condition. The two impressive viaducts here are both in need of repair, but for the purposes of the preservation project, only one of these structures will be required. Continuing through Chee Dale, this most impressive section which created considerable problems for the Victorian engineers who built the line, by having to be carved through solid rock, will present a relatively easy restoration task for the same reason. From Peak Forest Junction the Buxton branch is still used by B.R. for mineral traffic. At Buxton, planning permission has been obtained for the development of the derelict site of the former Midland station as the new terminus of the preserved railway. P.R.O. intend to create an important steam centre here and work towards this ultimate goal has already begun. Locomotives already on site at Buxton are a B.R. 9F 2-10-0 and an ex-L.M.S. Stanier 8F 2-8-0, both very suitable locomotives from classes which were once an everyday sight on the Peak Line.

One could be forgiven for thinking that such a project would be far too costly for an independent body to undertake successfully. However, the Peak Park Planning Board have purchased substantial sections of the disused trackbed and are considering seriously the granting of running rights for railway use. Peak Rail Operations Ltd., a public company, has now been incorporated to carry out the task of rebuilding the line and operating train services over the restored railway. A public share issue has already been made by the Company with the object of raising capital to undertake the first stages in the reconstruction of the Peak Railway, particularly the development of the Buxton site and the commencement of passenger services to Millers Dale. The project to rebuild the Peak Line was floated in 1975 with several objectives, the most important being the reopening of the Matlock–Buxton railway for the purpose of providing a full range of services including steam operation, weekday diesel commuter services for the benefit of the local population and also freight traffic, should the requirement arise. Importantly, the local authorities involved have stipulated that the provision of regular commuter services are an essential requirement which the railway company must fulfil if it is to receive their support.

The railway is to be rebuilt in stages as capital is raised, planning permission for development obtained, and physical obstacles overcome. The next few years should see several miles of line reopened for passenger services. Those station buildings and sites which remain available are being occupied by the railway company and rebuilt as one of the initial stages in the task of reconstruction. Locomotives are being acquired, these being mostly of types which were formerly common in this locality although the author has a stake in the ex-Great Western 4-6-0, 4936 'Kinlet Hall', which was purchased because of its generally sound mechanical condition. A start has been made towards the acquisition of suitable passenger stock and useful examples of goods vehicles. However, one of the tangible reminders of the growing strength of the project is its rapidly expanding membership which is rising towards a figure of 3,000. Support is being derived on a national scale and the project has even attracted interest from overseas. The scheme to rebuild the Peak Line is thus poised on the threshold of a very exciting future.

7. The Future

The way ahead is difficult to predict with accuracy since many factors could influence the course of events, particularly when one remembers that the preservation scheme is a long-term project which will take many years to complete. However, the general intentions of the promotors of the project can be assessed to obtain an insight into the kind of developments which are likely to take place in course of time. The basic structure of the railway management will comprise two separate organisations, these being the Peak Railway Society Ltd., a company limited by guarantee, which will provide the volunteer support, and Peak Rail Operations Ltd., a public company which will undertake the rebuilding of the railway and its operation thereafter.

The reopening of the line will be a phased operation commencing from the northern terminus and steam centre at Buxton and progressing southwards to Millers Dale and beyond. The initial phase of reconstruction will be a considerable step forward although it will take several years to complete. The commencement of services should provide an important stimulus to the generation of revenue which could be derived from the high levels of traffic which can reasonably be expected on the reopened section. A necessary function of Peak Rail Operations during this period will be to undertake a number of public share issues to raise a substantial proportion of the capital required to finance the phased reconstruction programme. Both the P.R.S. and P.R.O. are now considering a large number of other ideas for raising money to ensure that the Peak Line will become one of the major forces in private railway operation.

Further capital will be required for the purchase of locomotives and rolling stock. The task of procuring suitable steam locomotives is already well under way and further acquisitions are planned at the time of writing. The motive power policy of the P.R.O. favours large main line types which should be capable of handling the heavy traffic expected on this steeply graded line once services resume. The largest locomotives either destined for or actually resident on the line are a 9F 2-10-0, previously referred to, and a Southern West Country 4-6-2, 34101 'Hartland'. Further examples include the 8F 2-8-0 and G.W.R. Hall 4-6-0 together with a B.R. 2-6-4T. It is possible that further examples of L.M.S. and B.R. Standard types will be added to this fleet in due course. Main line diesels and DMUs may be acquired for the purpose of fulfilling the aim of running commuter traffic. Coaching stock is likely to consist primarily of B.R. Mk. 1 stock, but the purchase of more historically interesting vehicles is also likely.

One of the principal aims of the project is to recreate the former Midland/L.M.S. image of the railway and it is intended that the station buildings and other features should be rebuilt in such a fashion as to allow the visitor a means of interpreting the historical past of this important main line. In this way the restored railway will serve the functions of both a working line and a museum. It is hoped to be able to provide an interesting recreational activity for P.R.S. members, allowing them to run their own railways and teaching the new generations not only the railway heritage of Britain but the crafts and skills which permitted the creation and operation of railways in this country, valuable knowledge which could otherwise be completely lost in future years.

There can be little doubt that the Peak Railway will be a considerable advantage to the region in many respects. It should provide substantial economic benefits for the area by boosting shop and hotel income and increasing local employment in both service industries and on the railways itself which will require a proportion of full-time staff to operate it. The line could also become the foundation for transport in the area, providing connections with B.R. at both Matlock and Buxton. Very importantly, the Peak Railway would restore the present 'missing link' in the former Midland main line from Derby to Manchester, thereby reinstating the shortest rail route between the two cities. In addition, the railway would constitute an alternative to motor transport, thus helping to fulfil the aims of the Peak Park Planning Board in reducing the level of road traffic in the Peak District National Park.

The Peak Railway would be one of the longest privately operated lines in the country but the P.R.S./P.R.O organisation exists also for the purpose of covering possible closures of other B.R. lines which currently serve the Peak District communities. The P.R.O emphasis on financial strength is therefore of great importance in view of the real possibilities for further expansion of the existing project in order to maintain the dual connection with the B.R. network. The operation of Sunday Charter services from Matlock to Derby are a clear example of this policy. It is within the bounds of possibility that these services could eventually be operated with steam motive power if operational difficulties can be ironed out, thereby leading to the reality of steam hauled trains once again working out of Derby, the spiritual home of the Midland Railway.

One can see that the project to rebuild the Peak Line is one of the most ambitious preservation schemes ever planned. However, despite the enormity of the task, it does not appear that any of the hurdles should prove insurmountable. The rebuilding of the railway is certainly a long-term project, but to think of what could be achieved by the close of this century is a truly amazing prospect.

Train Schedules, Manchester to Derby and St. Pancras
Winter 1959—1960

		"Midland Pullman"	"Palatine"	4.35 Former "Peak Express"
Manchester Central	Dep.	8.50a.m.	2.25p.m.	4.35p.m.
Throstle Nest E. Junct.	Pass	8.54	2.29	4.39
Chorlton Junc.	Pass	8.57	2.32	4.43
Cheadle Heath	Arr.	9.03	Pass	Pass
	Dep.	9.04	2.37	4.48
New Mills S Junc.	Pass	9.15	2.48	5.00
Chinley	Arr.	Pass	2.53	Pass
	Dep.	9.18	2.55	5.05
Peak Forest	Pass	9.24	3.07	5.15
Millers Dale	Arr.	Pass	3.13	Pass
	Dep.	9.29	3.15	5.20
Rowsley	Pass	9.41	3.27½	5.31
Matlock	Arr.	Pass	3.32½	Pass
	Dep.	9.45	3.34½	5.35
Ambergate	Pass	9.54	3.44½	5.43
Derby North Junc.	Pass	10.04	—	—
Derby	Arr.	f	3.55	5.54
	Dep.		4.00	6.00
Spondon	Pass	10.12	—	—
Sheet Stores Junc.	Pass	10.19	4.11	6.12
Loughborough	Pass	10.26	4.19	Arr. 6.21 Dep. 6.23
Leicester	Arr.	Pass	4.32	6.38
	Dep.	10.37	4.36	6.42
Market Harborough	Pass	10.53	4.55	7.01
Desborough	Pass	10.58	5.01	7.07
Kettering	Pass	11.03	5.07	Arr. 7.14 Dep. 7.16
Wellingborough	Arr.	Pass	Pass	Pass
	Dep.	11.09	5.13	7.24
Milepost 59¾	Pass	11.14	5.19	7.30
Oakley	Pass	11.19	5.24	7.36
Bedford	Pass	11.22	5.27	7.39
Luton	Arr.	Pass	Pass	8.00
	Dep.	11.37	5.46	8.02
St Albans	Pass	11.45	5.55	8.14 *
Hendon	Pass	11.55	6.06	8.26
Kentish Town	Pass	12.00	6.12	8.32
St Pancras	Arr.	12.03 pm	6.15 pm	8.35 pm

f   to and from St Pancras via Chaddesden Avoiding Line

*   1 minute recovery time

Train Schedules, St. Pancras to Derby and Manchester
Winter 1959–1960

		"Palatine"	2.25 from St. Pancras	"Midland Pullman"
St. Pancras	Dep.	7.55 a.m.	2.25 p.m.	6.10 p.m.
Kentish Town	Pass	7.59	2.29	6.13
Hendon	Pass	8.05½	2.35½	6.18
St. Albans	Pass	8.18	2.48	6.28
Luton	Arr.	8.29	Pass	Pass
	Dep.	8.30	2.58	6.36
Bedford	Pass	8.48	3.14	6.51
Oakley	Pass	8.51	3.17	6.54
Milepost 59¾	Pass	8.57½	3.23½	7.00
Wellinborough	Arr.	9.04	Pass	Pass
	Dep.	9.06	3.28½	7.04
Kettering	Pass	9.14½	3.35	7.10
Desborough	Pass	9.21½	3.42	7.15
Market Harborough	Pass	9.26½	3.47	7.19
Leicester	Arr.	9.44	4.04	Pass
	Dep.	9.49	4.08	7.34
Loughborough	Pass	10.02	4.21	7.46
Sheet Stores Junc.	Pass	10.08½	4.27½	7.52
Spondon	Pass	–	–	7.59
Derby	Arr.	10.19	4.38	f
	Dep.	10.24	4.45	
Derby North Junc.	Pass	–	–	8.07
Ambergate	Pass	10.37	4.58	8.17
Matlock	Arr.	10.46	Pass	Pass
	Dep.	10.48	5.06	8.25
Rowsley	Pass	10.55	5.11	8.30
Millers Dale	Arr.	11.09	5.25	Pass
	Dep.	11.11	5.29	8.43
Peak Forest	Pass	11.20	5.38	8.49
Chinley	Arr.	Pass	Pass	Pass
	Dep.	11.26	5.44	8.55
New Mills S. Junc.	Pass	11.28½	5.46½	8.58
Cheadle Heath	Arr.	Pass	5.55½	9.07
	Dep.	11.36½	5.56½	9.08½
Chorlton Junc.	Pass	11.41	6.03	9.14
Throstle Nest E. Junc.	Pass	11.44	6.06	9.17
Manchester Central	Arr.	11.48 a.m.	6.10 p.m.	9.21 p.m.

f to Manchester via Chaddesden Avoiding Line

Distance and Speed Limits
Derby—Manchester

Mileposts: Up Side, from zero at St. Pancras via Chaddesden curve	Distance miles	* Speed limits m.p.h.
Derby	0.00	15
Derby North Junc. Box (U)	0.53 (a)	15 (b)
Nottingham Road	0.75	—
Little Eaton Junc. Box (U)	3.25	—
Duffield	5.25	70
Belper	7.80	—
Ambergate	10.35	25
Whatstandwell	12.30	40
High Peak Junc. Box (U)	13.40	55
Cromford	15.25	50
Matlock Bath	16.05	50
Matlock	17.15	—
Darley Dale	19.30	—
Rowsley	21.60	45
Bakewell	24.95	50
Great Longstone	27.30	60
Monsal Dale	28.70	60
Millers Dale	31.40	60
Millers Dale Junc. Box	32.70	35 (d)
Peak Forest Junc. Box (D)	33.20	(e)
Peak Forest	35.95	50 (f)
Chapel-en-le-Frith	39.65	70
Chinley	41.65	—
Buxworth	42.60	55
New Mills South Junc. Box (D)	44.35	70
Disley Box (D)	46.15	60 (c)
Hazel Grove	49.45	—
Cheadle Heath	53.45	70
Heaton Mersey	54.50	70
Didsbury	55.70	70
Withington	56.35	70
Chorlton Junc. Box	57.80	70
Chorlton-cum-Hardy	58.20	70
Throstle Nest East Junc. Box (D)	59.85	15
Manchester Central	61.35	—

KEY:—

*	70 m.p.h. and under.
(a)	From St. Pancras via Chaddesden (Avoiding Derby Station), 128.40 miles.
(b)	To and from Chaddesden avoiding line only.
(c)	Through Disley Tunnel.
(d)	Down line only.
(e)	50 m.p.h. down; 60 m.p.h. up.
(f)	Through Dove Holes Tunnel.
U	Up side of line.
D	Down.